THE PSYCHOLOGY OF
THE LAST OF US

THE PSYCHOLOGY OF
THE LAST OF US

EDITED BY ANTHONY M. BEAN, PHD

Leyline Publishing, Inc.
Fort Worth, TX

THIS PUBLICATION IS UNOFFICIAL AND UNATHORIZED. IT HAS NOT BEEN PREPARED, APPROVED, AUTHORIZED, LICENSED OR ENDORSED BY ANY ENTITY THAT CREATED OR PRODUCED THE WELL-KNOWN NAUGHTY DOG, HBO, OR THEIR AFFLIATES

Book and *"The Last of Us*: A Masterpiece of Emotional Storytelling" © 2024 by Anthony M. Bean

"The Uncontrollable Mutineer: Fungi and Fear in *The Last of Us*" © 2024 by Henry St. Leger

"A Bond Worth More Than All the World: The Role of Adoption in *The Last of Us*" © 2024 by Amanda Duncan and Bryan Duncan

"Alcohol and Rags: The Consequences of Violent Agency in a Digital World" © 2024 by Roy Wang

"The Narrative of Trauma: How *The Last of Us* Portrays PTSD and Trauma" © 2024 by Michelle "Michie" Leccese

"Look for the Light: Surviving Grief in a World Gone Dark" © 2024 by Daniel Kaufmann

"The Rest of Us: How Queer Youth Find Themselves When No One Helps Them Look" © 2024 by Kenneth Shepard

"Navigating Posttraumatic Growth in *The Last of Us* Fandom: The Power of One-Sided Connections" © 2024 by Adam Baldowski

"Bill and Frank Endured so Bill and Frank Could Love" © 2024 by Charalambos "Harry" Loizides

"The Loss of Us: A Psychoanalytic View of Loss and Love in *The Last of Us* Games" © 2024 by Angelo Mirra

"Metamorphosis: Preserving Life's Magic Against the Backdrop of Tragedy" © 2024 by Tyler W. Secor

"Finding the 'Why': Resilience Through the Eyes of *The Last of Us*" © 2024 by Melinda Korte

"Surviving the Zombie Apocalypse: Examining What *The Last of Us* Teaches About Struggle and Rising Above" © 2024 by Kat Jaeger and Tony Jaeger

All rights reserved. No part of this book may be used or reproduced in any manner whatsoever without prior written permission, except for brief quotation of less than one hundred (100) words for reviews and articles.

Leyline Publishing, Inc.
7801 Oakmont Blvd, Suite 101
Fort Worth, Texas 76132
leylinepublishing.com | geektherapeutics.com

Printed in the United States of America

10 9 8 7 6 5 4 3 2 1

Library of Congress Cataloging-in-Publication Data is available upon request.

978-1-955406-29-1 (trade paper)
978-1-955406-30-7 (e-book)
978-1-955406-31-4 (Audio Book)

Editing by Anthony M. Bean
Copyediting and Proofreading by Kate Hollis
Text Design and composition by Asya Blue
Cover Design and Illustration by Arianna "Kaz" Unciano

To those who wander through the shadows of the mind, seeking light in the darkest corners. This work is dedicated to the survivors of their own battles, the seekers of truth, and the believers in the resilience of the human spirit. May you find strength in your journey and solace in understanding. This book is for you, the warriors of the mind, the architects of hope, and the guardians of humanity's enduring spirit.

CONTENTS

THE LAST OF US:
A MASTERPIECE OF EMOTIONAL STORYTELLING
Anthony M. Bean | 1

THE UNCONTROLLABLE MUTINEER:
FUNGI AND FEAR IN *THE LAST OF US*
Henry St Leger | 19

LOOK FOR THE LIGHT: SURVIVING GRIEF
IN A WORLD GONE DARK
Daniel Kaufmann | 33

A BOND WORTH MORE THAN ALL THE WORLD:
THE ROLE OF ADOPTION IN *THE LAST OF US*
Amanda Duncan and Bryan Duncan | 55

ALCOHOL AND RAGS:
THE CONSEQUENCES OF VIOLENT AGENCY
IN A DIGITAL WORLD
Roy Wang | 69

NAVIGATING POSTTRAUMATIC GROWTH
IN *THE LAST OF US* FANDOM:
THE POWER OF ONE-SIDED CONNECTIONS
Adam Baldowski | 85

THE NARRATIVE OF TRAUMA:
HOW *THE LAST OF US* PORTRAYS PTSD AND TRAUMA
Michelle "Michie" Leccese | 101

THE REST OF US:
HOW QUEER YOUTH FIND THEMSELVES WHEN
NO ONE HELPS THEM LOOK
Kenneth Shepard | 121

BILL AND FRANK ENDURED SO BILL AND
FRANK COULD LOVE
Charalambos "Harry" Loizides | 135

THE LOSS OF US:
A PSYCHOANALYTIC VIEW OF LOSS
AND LOVE IN THE LAST OF US GAMES
Angelo Mirra | 153

METAMORPHOSIS:
PRESERVING LIFE'S MAGIC AGAINST
THE BACKDROP OF TRAGEDY
Tyler W. Secor | 167

FINDING THE 'WHY':
RESILIENCE THROUGH THE EYES OF
THE LAST OF US
Melinda Korte | 185

SURVIVING THE ZOMBIE APOCALYPSE:
EXAMINING WHAT *THE LAST OF US*
TEACHES ABOUT STRUGGLE AND RISING ABOVE
Kat Jaeger and Tony Jaeger | 205

THE LAST OF US: A MASTERPIECE OF EMOTIONAL STORYTELLING

ANTHONY M. BEAN

Video games have undergone a remarkable transformation from simple, pixelated pastimes to immersive experiences that rival film and literature. This evolution has been driven by advancements in technology, storytelling, and game design, enabling video games to evoke a wide range of emotions and provide compelling, atmospheric experiences for players. One exemplary title that embodies this evolution is *The Last of Us*, a critically acclaimed game developed by Naughty Dog.

Technological advancements in video game hardware and software have played a pivotal role in enhancing the immersive capabilities of the medium. Modern video game consoles and gaming PCs are equipped with powerful graphics processors, high-definition displays, and surround sound systems capable of rendering detailed and lifelike environments. These advancements enable developers to create richly immersive worlds that captivate players' senses and draw them into the game experience. In *The Last of Us*, the meticulously crafted environments, realistic character animations, and atmospheric sound design work together to create a sense of realism and presence that deeply immerses players in the post-apocalyptic world.

Moreover, the evolution of storytelling in video games has contributed to their ability to evoke emotions and engage players on a deeper level. Gone are the days of simple plots and one-dimensional characters; modern video games feature complex narratives, multidimensional characters, and branching storylines that allow players to shape the outcome of the game through their choices and actions. In *The Last of Us*, the narrative is driven by compelling characters, such as Joel and Ellie, whose emotional journeys resonate with players long after they put down the controller. The game's masterful storytelling, filled with poignant moments of triumph and tragedy, creates an emotionally resonant experience that stays with players long after they complete the game.

The interactive nature of video games distinguishes them from more passive forms of entertainment (such as film or television), allowing players to actively participate in the narrative and shape their own experiences. This interactivity fosters a sense of agency and investment in the game world, as players become personally involved in the outcomes of their actions. In *The Last of Us*, players are not mere spectators, but active participants in Joel and Ellie's journey, making life-and-death decisions and experiencing the consequences of their choices firsthand. This level of interactivity creates a deeply immersive and emotionally engaging experience that is unique to the medium of video games. *The Last of Us* exemplifies this evolution, with its richly immersive world, compelling narrative, and emotionally resonant characters.

 IMMERSED IN SURVIVAL: THE UNMATCHED PRESENCE OF *THE LAST OF US*

In both the video game and TV show versions of *The Last of Us*, the creators expertly craft an atmospheric environs that envelops players and viewers within a haunting post-apocalyptic world.

THE LAST OF US: A MASTERPIECE OF EMOTIONAL STORYTELLING

Through meticulous attention to detail, both mediums offer players and viewers a profound sense that they themselves are truly within the world of *The Last of Us*. In the video game, players inhabit virtual landscapes teeming with intricate environments and atmospheric details. Every abandoned building, overgrown street, and decaying structure tells a story, drawing players deeper into the desolate world. Similarly, the TV show meticulously recreates the gritty aesthetic of the game, with lush cinematography and immersive set design that transport viewers to the heart of the apocalypse.

Advancements in technology, such as virtual reality (VR), create a level of immersion that is unprecedented in the video game industry. VR technology allows players to step directly into the shoes of characters like Joel and Ellie, experiencing the world of *The Last of Us* in stunning detail. As players don VR headsets and wield motion controllers, they are fully immersed in the harrowing journey, with every movement and action feeling palpably real. The game manages to effectively blur the line between reality and fiction, immersing players in a visceral experience unlike any other.

In essence, *The Last of Us* video game and TV show masterfully utilize immersive techniques and technologies to transport players and viewers into a world ravaged by infection and despair. Through meticulous attention to detail, advancements in technology, and the power of social connection, both mediums create an immersive experience that lingers long after the screen fades to black.

FLOWING THROUGH THE APOCALYPSE: MASTERING THE FLOW STATE IN *THE LAST OF US*

The Last of Us video game, and its adaptation into a TV show, exemplify the concept of the flow state— a psychological state of complete immersion and engagement in an activity. This concept, critical to understanding player and viewer engagement, is brilliantly executed in both formats.

In the realm of the video game, *The Last of Us* crafts a meticulously balanced environment that seamlessly blends challenge with skill. Players are continuously presented with scenarios that test their strategic thinking, adaptability, and quick reflexes; yet the game equips them with the necessary skills and tools to navigate these challenges effectively. This equilibrium is vital for sustaining a flow state, as it prevents players from feeling overwhelmed or under challenged. The game's design — encompassing clear goals, immediate feedback, and a sense of progression — furthers this state of flow. Players are rewarded with a tangible sense of achievement as they accomplish objectives and overcome obstacles, reinforcing their engagement and pushing them deeper into the immersive world of *The Last of Us*.

Similarly, the narrative structure and pacing of the TV show are carefully curated to draw viewers into a state of flow. Through expert storytelling, the show maintains a delicate balance between tension and resolution, mirroring the game's challenge-skill balance. Each episode weaves suspense, emotional depth, and character arcs in a manner that makes viewers eager for more through satisfying narrative progressions. The show's ability to keep the audience fully absorbed is akin to the video game's engagement strategy, creating a continuous loop of engagement that encourages viewers to become deeply invested in the unfolding story.

The Last of Us extends the concept of flow beyond traditional gameplay into the emotional realm. Both the game and the TV show delve into the complexities of human emotion, relationships, and survival, fostering a meaningful emotional connection between the audience and the characters. This connection is essential for maintaining flow, as players and viewers become so emotionally invested in the characters' journeys that their sense of time and reality begins to blur. The challenges faced by Joel and Ellie resonate on a personal level, making every success and failure feel intimately real — and thus drawing the audience deeper into a state of flow.

The immersive world of *The Last of Us* is further enriched by its atmospheric elements—detailed environments, sound design, and visual storytelling—which all serve to heighten the sense of presence. In the video game, players are not just navigating a digital world; they are inhabiting it, with every texture, sound, and interaction designed to enhance realism and immersion. The TV show translates these elements into visual and auditory cues that build a vivid post-apocalyptic landscape for viewers, making the experience of watching the show as immersive as playing the game.

The impact of achieving a flow state in *The Last of Us* extends beyond mere entertainment. For players, it enhances cognitive abilities, problem-solving skills, and emotional resilience, as they navigate the game's challenges. For TV viewers, it deepens empathy and understanding, as they are drawn into the characters' emotional struggles and moral dilemmas. This profound engagement leads to increased enjoyment, enhanced performance in gameplay, and greater intrinsic motivation to continue exploring the story of *The Last of Us*.

The Last of Us video game and TV show stand as paragons of creating and sustaining a flow state in interactive and narrative media. By expertly balancing challenge and skill, weaving compelling stories, and fostering deep emotional connections, they provide players and viewers with an unparalleled immersive experience. This mastery over the flow state not only makes *The Last of Us* a memorable journey, but also showcases the potential of video games and their adaptations to deeply engage and affect their audiences.

BEYOND SURVIVAL: THE DEEP EMOTIONAL ENGAGEMENT OF *THE LAST OF US*

The Last of Us video game and TV show masterfully evoke emotional engagement, drawing players and viewers into a profound emotional journey that lingers well beyond the screen. Through a combination of narrative storytelling, character development, and immersive world-building, both mediums create a rich tapestry of emotional experiences that resonate deeply with the audience.

Narrative storytelling is at the heart of *The Last of Us*, weaving a compelling tale of survival, loss, and hope that pulls the audience into its world. The game and show alike utilize storytelling to craft a narrative that is both engaging and emotionally charged. Through the journey of Joel and Ellie, the audience is presented with a story that explores the depths of human resilience and the complexities of relationships in a world gone to ruin. Memorable moments, from poignant conversations to heart-wrenching decisions, are framed within a narrative that challenges the audience's emotions at every turn. Unexpected plot twists and revelations ensure that the emotional journey is as unpredictable as it is captivating, making the narrative a powerful vehicle for emotional engagement.

Character development further enhances the emotional depth of *The Last of Us*. Joel and Ellie, along with a cast of well-realized supporting characters, are portrayed with such complexity and nuance that they transcend their fictional existence. Each character's distinct personality, motivations, and evolution over the course of the story make them relatable and deeply human. The audience forms strong emotional attachments to these characters, celebrating their triumphs and mourning their losses. This connection is key to the emotional engagement of *The Last of Us*, as it transforms the characters' journey into a deeply personal experience for the audience.

The immersive gameplay experiences of the video game, and the immersive atmosphere of the TV show, play critical roles in evoking emotional engagement. The game's dynamic environments, atmospheric sound design, and realistic graphics immerse players in the post-apocalyptic world of *The Last of Us*, making every encounter, discovery, and challenge feel immediate and impactful. Similarly, the TV show's visual storytelling, coupled with its faithful recreation of the game's aesthetic and mood, draws viewers into the same immersive world. The sense of presence these elements create enhances the emotional impact of the narrative and character arcs, making moments of triumph, tension, and tragedy all the more powerful. The audience is not just observing the story unfold; they are living it, with every victory feeling earned and every loss feeling personal.

The Last of Us video game and TV show are prime examples of emotional engagement in media. Through the interplay of narrative storytelling, character development, and immersive experiences, they evoke a spectrum of emotions from their audience, from the highest highs to the lowest lows. This emotional engagement is not just a testament to the quality of the storytelling and design, but also to the power of video games (and their adaptations) to connect with audiences on a deeply emotional level.

ECHOES OF HUMANITY: THE RELATABLE CHARACTERS OF *THE LAST OF US*

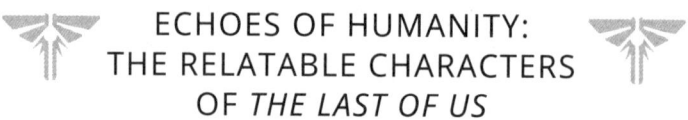

The Last of Us video game and TV show excel in crafting relatable characters. Joel and Ellie, the central figures of the narrative, are so intricately drawn that they transcend their character roles and become real, relatable beings. Joel's portrayal as a grizzled survivor burdened by loss, and Ellie's depiction as a brave yet vulnerable teenager forced to grow up too quickly, offer a nuanced exploration of their personalities and inner struggles. This depth allows audiences to see parts of themselves in Joel and Ellie, making their journey not just a tale of survival, but a deeply personal experience.

The evolution of Joel and Ellie's relationship is the foundation of the story, intricately woven through their shared experiences in the desolate world they navigate. The progression from mutual distrust to a deep, familial bond is portrayed with a realism that speaks to the complexities of human relationships. Their interactions, filled with moments of care, conflict, and growth, reveal the layered dynamics of their relationship, offering a poignant look at how adversity can forge unbreakable bonds. This development is key to engaging the audience, as it mirrors the ups and downs of real human connections, making the emotional stakes of their journey feel incredibly real and relatable.

The inclusion of a diverse ensemble of supporting characters further enriches the narrative landscape of *The Last of Us*. Characters such as Tess, with her steadfast resolve, and Bill, with his secretive nature, are not mere side notes, but central to the story, each bringing their own stories and perspectives. These characters are crafted with the same attention to detail and complexity as the protagonists, providing a multifaceted view of the world and its inhabitants. Through their interactions with Joel and Ellie, they reveal different facets of survival and humanity, expanding and enriching the narrative. Their presence not only enhances the world-building, but also offers varied lenses through which the audience can explore the themes of the story, making the narrative experience all the richer and engaging.

Through masterful writing and character development, *The Last of Us* video game and TV show create a compelling narrative filled with characters who are not only relatable, but also deeply human. The journey of Joel, Ellie, and the cast of characters they meet along the way, captivates the audience, inviting them to reflect on their own experiences and emotions. This approach to storytelling, where characters are portrayed with depth, complexity, and genuine emotion, is what makes *The Last of Us* a standout example of character-driven narrative in both gaming and television.

 HEART OF THE APOCALYPSE: THE EMOTIONAL ODYSSEY OF *THE LAST OF US*

The Last of Us video game and TV show stand as monumental achievements in storytelling, profoundly impacting players and viewers with their deep emotional content. By weaving themes of loss, survival, and the intricacies of human relationships into the fabric of their narratives, they craft an emotional journey that resonates on a universal level, leaving a lasting impression on those who journey through their post-apocalyptic world.

At the core of *The Last of Us* is its unparalleled ability to evoke a spectrum of emotions, skillfully balancing moments of tender human connection against the backdrop of a brutal, unforgiving world. These narratives invite audiences into the lives of Joel and Ellie, allowing them to share in their moments of joy, sorrow, fear, and hope. This emotional investment is crucial, transforming the game and show from mere entertainment into a deeply personal experience. Scenes of quiet intimacy a shared joke, or a silent exchange of understanding — are as compelling as the intense, adrenaline-fueled encounters with dangers lurking in their world. This balance keeps the audience emotionally engaged, riding alongside the characters through every twist and turn of their journey.

Enhancing the emotional depth of *The Last of Us* are its audio-visual elements, which play a pivotal role in immersing players and viewers in its emotionally charged atmosphere. The remarkable attention to detail in character design and animation allows for a range of expressions that convey the subtlest nuances of emotion, making the characters' experiences feel real and immediate. The game and show's environments are meticulously crafted, from the haunting beauty of nature reclaiming civilization to the desolation of abandoned cities, each setting enriches the narrative, lending an atmospheric depth that heightens the emotional impact.

Composer Gustavo Santaolalla's hauntingly beautiful score is another element that significantly amplifies the emotional landscape of *The Last of Us*. The music acts as an emotional conduit, weaving through the narrative and evoking a profound response from the audience. From the melancholic strains of the guitar to the suspenseful undertones that underscore moments of danger, the score is a constant presence, shaping the emotional contour of the story and deepening the audience's immersion in the world.

Furthermore, *The Last of Us* bravely confronts the darker aspects of humanity, presenting players and viewers with dilemmas that challenge moral conventions and provoke introspection. The narrative does not shy away from exploring the consequences of violence, the pain of loss, and the complexity of moral choices in a world where the lines between right and wrong are blurred. These themes are handled with a thoughtfulness that respects the audience's intelligence, prompting them to consider their own beliefs and values. This exploration of moral ambiguity and human resilience adds a profound layer to the narrative, enriching the emotional experience and fostering a deeper connection with the characters and their plight.

By engaging the audience on multiple levels— through emotion, logic, and audiovisual input—*The Last of Us* transcends the boundaries of its mediums, becoming more than just a story about survival in a post-apocalyptic world. It becomes a reflection on the human condition, a commentary on the capacity for love, sacrifice, and endurance in the face of unimaginable challenges. The emotional content of *The Last of Us* does not just leave a lasting impact on its audience; it invites them to grow, to empathize, and to reflect, making it an unforgettable journey that resonates long after the final credits roll.

 HEARTBEATS IN THE RUINS: NAVIGATING THE EMOTIONAL LANDSCAPE OF *THE LAST OF US*

The Last of Us video game has had a profound impact on many players, eliciting strong emotional responses and sparking discussions about its themes and characters. Players often report feeling a deep connection to the story and its characters, with some even describing the game as a transformative experience. The emotional resonance of *The Last of Us* stems from its relatable characters, compelling writing, and immersive gameplay experiences, which combine to create a uniquely immersive and emotionally engaging experience for players.

Moreover, the game's exploration of universal themes — such as love, loss, and redemption — resonates with players on a personal level, allowing them to find meaning and relevance in the game's narrative. Whether it is the bond between Joel and Ellie, the struggle for survival in a hostile world, or the quest for hope in the face of despair, *The Last of Us* speaks to fundamental aspects of the human experience that are universally understood and appreciated.

The Last of Us encourages players to empathize with its characters and consider the moral and ethical implications of their actions. By confronting players with difficult choices and complex dilemmas, the game challenges them to think critically about their own values and beliefs, fostering empathy, introspection, and personal growth in the process. The emotional resonance of *The Last of Us* extends beyond the confines of the game itself, inspiring deep reflections and conversations among players about its themes, characters, and impact on society as a whole.

 SHADES OF RIGHT: THE MORAL QUANDARIES OF *THE LAST OF US*

The game's moral dilemmas and ambiguous characters prompt players to reflect on their own values and beliefs, challenging them to make difficult decisions with far-reaching consequences. This moral complexity adds depth to the gameplay experience and encourages players to consider the ethical implications of their actions. Throughout the game, players are presented with choices that force them to weigh the needs of the individual against the greater good, leading to moments of moral ambiguity and uncertainty.

Moreover, *The Last of Us* explores the consequences of violence and the cycle of revenge, prompting players to consider the human cost of their actions. The game's portrayal of violence is not gratuitous; it serves a strategic, narrative purpose, highlighting the brutal realities of survival in a post-apocalyptic world and the toll it takes on its characters. By confronting players with the consequences of their actions, *The Last of Us* encourages them to think critically about the role of violence in society and the ethical implications of their choices.

The game's morally ambiguous characters challenge players' preconceived notions of right and wrong, forcing them to confront the complexities of the human condition. Characters such as Joel, Ellie, and their allies and adversaries are neither wholly good nor wholly evil — but instead exist in shades of gray, reflecting the moral ambiguity of the world they inhabit. By presenting players with characters who are flawed and morally complex, *The Last of Us* encourages them to question their assumptions and consider the perspectives of others, fostering empathy, understanding, and tolerance in the process.

THROUGH THEIR EYES: EMPATHY AND PERSPECTIVE IN *THE LAST OF US*

Through its immersive storytelling and relatable characters, *The Last of Us* fosters empathy and perspective-taking in players. By stepping into the shoes of Joel or Ellie, players gain insight into the struggles of others and develop a greater appreciation for the complexities of the human experience. The game's narrative encourages players to empathize with its characters and consider the world from their perspective, fostering a sense of connection and understanding that transcends the boundaries of the game itself.

Moreover, *The Last of Us* challenges players to confront difficult emotions and confrontations, forcing them to navigate complex moral dilemmas and make difficult decisions with far-reaching consequences. By engaging players on an emotional and intellectual level, the game encourages empathy, introspection, and personal growth, leaving a lasting impact long after the credits have rolled.

The Last of Us inspires players to consider the broader implications of its themes and characters, sparking discussions and reflections about issues such as love, loss, and the human condition. Through its immersive storytelling and thought-provoking gameplay experiences, the game invites players to explore fundamental aspects of the human experience and consider their own values and beliefs in the process. By fostering empathy, perspective-taking, and critical thinking, *The Last of Us* transcends the boundaries of traditional entertainment and leaves a lasting impact on players.

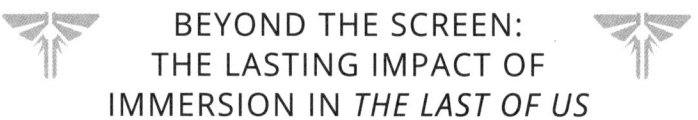

BEYOND THE SCREEN: THE LASTING IMPACT OF IMMERSION IN *THE LAST OF US*

Immersive storytelling stands at the core of *The Last of Us*, elevating it from a mere game to an emotionally charged narrative experience. In the desolate, post-apocalyptic world that Naughty Dog has meticulously crafted, every dilapidated building, every whispered conversation, and every desperate fight for survival serves to pull the player further into the game's universe. This depth of immersion makes the player's journey through the game not just about surviving but about experiencing the story's emotional highs and lows as if they were their own.

The immersive storytelling of *The Last of Us* is also pivotal in conveying the game's complex themes, such as loss, hope, and the moral ambiguities of survival. By intimately experiencing Joel and Ellie's journey, players are compelled to confront these themes head-on, leading to moments of introspection and emotional reflection that are rare in other forms of media. This is storytelling that not only entertains, but resonates on a deeply personal level, challenging players to consider what they would do in the characters' places. The game's ability to blend narrative and gameplay so seamlessly ensures that the story's impact is felt with every action taken and obstacle overcome.

The player's emotional investment in the characters and their fates drives players to think about the game's events and decisions even when they're not playing, leading to discussions, fan theories, and a strong community bond around the game. This level of engagement is the hallmark of a masterpiece in gaming, demonstrating the power of immersive storytelling to not only entertain but also unite and inspire. Through its masterful blend of narrative depth, character development, and interactive gameplay, *The Last of Us* sets a benchmark for what video games can achieve as a storytelling medium.

The Last of Us stands as a testament to the power of video games as a storytelling medium. Through its relatable characters, compelling writing, and emotional content, the game captivates players and invites them to explore complex themes and moral dilemmas. By examining the psychology behind video games and the impact of *The Last of Us* on players, we gain a deeper understanding of the profound influence that video games can have on individuals and society as a whole.

About the Author

ANTHONY M. BEAN, PHD, Licensed Psychologist, CEO of Geek Therapeutics, has become a sought-after expert in the media, regularly contributing his insights on various psychological topics. With a dynamic and engaging presence, he has been featured on numerous platforms, including podcasts, TV shows, and radio programs. Whether discussing video game addiction, mental health, or therapeutic interventions, Dr. Bean's media appearances are characterized by his ability to distill complex concepts into accessible and relatable insights. His articulate and personable approach makes him a trusted source for understanding psychological issues in the modern world, resonating with audiences seeking expert perspectives in an easily digestible format. Dr. Bean's research endeavors reflect a commitment to advancing the understanding of complex psychological phenomena. With a focus on contemporary issues, his work spans diverse areas such as video game addiction, therapeutic interventions, and the intersection of technology and mental health. Dr. Bean employs rigorous methodologies, incorporating both quantitative and qualitative approaches to gather nuanced insights. His research contributions not only expand the academic discourse but also have practical implications for individuals and professionals alike. Through a dedication to evidence-based exploration, Dr. Bean's research endeavors contribute significantly to the evolving landscape of psychology, shedding light on crucial aspects of modern-day challenges and therapeutic solutions.

References

Banks, J. (2015). *Object, Me, Symbiote, Other: A social typology of player-avatar relationships.* First Monday, 20, 2.

Bean, A., & Groth-Marnat, G. (2014). Video gamers and personality: A five-factor model to understand game playing style. *Psychology of Popular Media Culture,* 5(1), 27–38. https://doi.org/10.1037/ppm0000025

Lewis, M. L., Weber, R., & Bowman, N. D. (2008). They May Be Pixels, But They're MY Pixels: Developing a Metric of Character Attachment in Role-Playing Video Games. *Cyberpsychology and Behavior,* 11, 4, 515-518.

Oliver, M. B., Bowman, N. D., Woolley, J. K., Rogers, R., Sherrick, B. I., & Chung, M.-Y. (2015). Video games as meaningful entertainment experiences. *Psychology of Popular Media Culture,* 5, 4, 390-405.

Posey, J. (2013). *Tastes like chicken: Authenticity in a totally fake world.* at

http://schedule2013.gdconf.com/session-id/823740. Presented at the Game

Developers Conference, San Francisco, CA.

Reeves, B., & Nass, C. (2006). *The media equation: How people treat computers, television, and new media like real people and places.* Stanford, Calif: CSLI Publ.

Turkle, S., & Simon & Schuster. (2014). *Life on the screen: Identity in the age of the Internet.*

New York: Simon & Schuster Paperbacks.

THE UNCONTROLLABLE MUTINEER: FUNGI AND FEAR IN *THE LAST OF US*

HENRY ST LEGER

"How is it that you're never scared?" —Sam

"Who says that I'm not?" —Ellie

The zombie apocalypse was hardly a new idea by the time *The Last of Us* released on the PlayStation 3 – even in the world of video games.

In the 1980s, the world saw *The Evil Dead* release on the Commodore 64, and *Zombie Zombie* on ZX Spectrum. In the 90s, there was *Horror Zombie from the Crypt* on the Amiga and Atari ST, *Zombie Nation* on the NES, the arcade game series *The House of the Dead*, and the start of the *Resident Evil* games. In the early 2000s, there was everything from console and PC game *Left 4 Dead* to *Little Red Riding Hood's Zombie BBQ* on the Nintendo DS.

The Last of Us did not grace our consoles until 2013 – the same year we saw the release of a cartoonish parody of the genre, *Plants vs Zombies 2*. This offers strong evidence that the zombie apocalypse had, like an undead ghoul with nothing to feed on, pretty much run out of steam by that point, at least in the medium of video games.

As ever, though, genres have a way of evolving with the times, and the zombie itself has proven surprisingly elastic – morphing from its origins in Haitian folklore to a blockbuster movie stalwart. It served as an allegory for the horrors of war (*Night of the Living Dead*) and mindless shopping mall consumerism (*Dawn of the Dead*), and even an indie darling (*Life After Beth*) or romcom hero (*Warm Bodies*). With *The Last of Us* we saw another pivot for the humble zombie at an opportune time –something that reshaped our conception of what a zombie apocalypse could be, and where it could come from.

I am talking, of course, about fungi.

 ## FUNGI: GOOD OR BAD?

The bestselling 2013 game *The Last Of Us* takes place in a crumbled American landscape, where the spread of the cordyceps fungus has killed or transformed a vast amount of the nation's population, in an apocalyptic fable that realizes our fears of uncontrolled, catastrophic contamination.

The Last of Us is a story with many familiar themes for a zombie apocalypse. It begins with a sudden outbreak, as Joel flees infected neighbors with his brother Tommy and daughter Sarah, escalates into conflict marked by antagonism between mindless undead and soldiers who are" just following orders." Amidst waves of horrifying ghouls that must be held off at every turn, a hardened older man shepherds a young girl to safety, opening his heart in the process. There is immense loss by the time the credits roll.

However, the introduction of fungi makes these tropes feel altogether quite different – our collective mycophobia, or fear of fungi, renders the undead in new and vivid ways. These infected beings are not reanimated by magics or mad scientists, but through the natural evolution of a real-life fungus — inspired by a now-famous segment of the nature documentary *Planet Earth*.

Ophiocordyceps unilateralis – handily shortened to 'cordyceps' – is best known for infecting ants and controlling their movements, and is predominantly found in tropical forests across Southeast Asia, alongside those in Brazil and Central America.

As reported in National Geographic, "The *Ophiocordyceps unilateralis* fungus has just one goal: self-propagation and dispersal. Researchers think the fungus, found in tropical forests, infects a foraging ant through spores that attach and penetrate the exoskeleton and slowly takes over its behavior."

This strain of tropical, parasitic fungus uses "bioactive compounds" to "interfere with the ant's nervous system and control hosts directly at the muscles," and is able to steer the ant away from its nest and towards a place more conducive for propagating the fungus further. Eventually, the ant dies, and the fungus expands out of the ant's body, emitting spores to infect the next round of victims.

The Last of Us game director Bruce Straley says in a VentureBeat interview that he and Neil Druckmann, the game's creative director, "would watch these videos where they literally use the term 'zombie ants.' That was our jumping-off point."

The human body is no stranger to fungi. Countless people experience fungal infections of some kind – from thrush to athlete's foot – and our increase in mycelial knowledge means that fungi are increasingly on the mind. One 1996 research paper, in the journal *Mycoses*, points to a growing association in medical literature between human disease and fungi – while another in the same journal concludes that misdiagnosed fungal infections were causing more patients to develop phobias of fungus overall.

However, there are legitimate reasons to be wary of fungi. One 2020 research paper in the medical journal *Microbial Cell* estimates that 1.7 million people are killed by fungi every year – more than those caused by either tuberculosis or malaria – and that "over 150 million severe cases of fungal infection occur worldwide."

The flesh-eating mucormycosis (also known as black fungus) can be found in rotting leaves, wood, or soil, and if untreated can infect the brain, trigger seizures, and prove terminal – while a cryptococcus neoformans infection can have the same symptoms as pneumonia or meningitis. These fungi are relatively rare in humans, but are also potentially life-threatening where they do appear.

While a worldwide zombie pandemic is unlikely – the average temperature of the human body makes it inhospitable to cordyceps– killer fungus is very much already with us, and impacting the human population on a notable scale.

The Last of Us draws on this potential deadliness, using real-life examples from nature (the zombie ants) as well as our uncertain, uneasy proximity to mycelial growth – knitting together a semi-plausible exaggeration of existing fears. The show ditches supernatural plot points for ones that reflect the dangers of the natural world.

Fungi can be safe to eat, or deathly poisonous; food, or a sign that food is rotting and expired. When foraging, it is often hard to tell by sight which one a particular mushroom may be – a fact that causes countless people fall ill every year. The hallucinogenic properties of certain mushrooms (e.g. psilocybin, the fungus-derived hallucinogenic) can also go both ways: a transcendental experience for a human, or the method by which an insect brain is flooded and overwhelmed. A good trip, or a very, very bad one. Some strains of parasitic cordyceps can even be safe for humans to eat in small doses, and are increasingly used in homeopathic supplements.

This duality of mushrooms is also something that turns up repeatedly in some of the biggest gaming franchises today. The *Super Mario Bros.* games contain mushrooms that can make you

THE UNCONTROLLABLE MUTINEER: FUNGI AND FEAR IN THE LAST OF US

grow bigger or stronger, as well as other kinds that can knock you down for size or kill you outright. Characters inspired by mushrooms can be friends (Toad) or foe (Goomba). In the popular role-playing game *Dungeons & Dragons*, too, players can take on the mantle of a Spores Druid, a worshipper of the natural world that uses fungal spores to harm, heal, and control other creatures – neither good nor bad, but a third muddied category, capable of both.

This complexity adds a thick layer of unease to the action in *The Last of Us*, as we evade, attack, or succumb to zombies embedded within the earth's natural mycelial network. Fungi feel like both friend and foe, familiar and alien; the outline of a human figure that could be either alive or undead. This is a recurring theme throughout *The Last of Us* — we wonder if the young boy Sam, rocking on the edge of his bed after a zombie bite, is just a nervous child until the camera pans around to his infected face. We also question Ellie; once-infected, but seemingly immune, clean and carrier at once.

DISGUST IS INSTRUCTIVE

Crucially, fungus is also associated with rot – food that has been soiled, contaminated. In the opening level of *The Last of Us*, any players exploring the bathroom can inspect a newspaper with the headline "FDA EXPANDS LIST OF CONTAMINATED CROPS," putting the blame for the zombie outbreak on crops where mold and fungus proliferate.

In the late-game cannibal camp, Ellie is touted as possible food for her captors until she reveals her dormant infection, and to them her body becomes spoiled food. The fungus and the zombie are a singular unclean organism, merging rotten food and rotten flesh, continually provoking our disgust.

Disgust is inherently instructive: it tells us instinctively what to avoid, and what not to touch or eat. It is a feeling that fuels the game's survival horror, and keeps us moving slowly through the game's many stealth sections, crumbled office buildings, underground sewers, or the open road — desperate to evade the touch of unclean things.

In *The Last of Us*, contamination is around every corner – and as survivors, our playable characters are eternally vigilant about exposure, distancing themselves from unclean creatures and donning gas masks to keep out poisonous spores. Even the immune Ellie is not exempt from danger. A single bite can be an immediate death sentence, tearing out the character's throat. Outside the rush of combat, infected characters (like the 13-year-old Sam, who becomes a zombie overnight) can turn in a matter of hours and prove a danger to the protagonists' well-being once again.

It was painfully fitting for *The Last of Us: Part II*, a long-awaited sequel, to release midway through 2020, when countless countries around the globe were navigating lockdowns and widespread health anxiety around the novel Covid-19 virus. As people grappled with official guidance around social distancing or masking, they developed additional, maladaptive behaviors like washing vegetables in detergent.

Part of the game's resonance, if not its success, could lie in how it articulates the fear of contamination that comes amid viral outbreaks, channeling that anxiety into the careful vigilance of a stealth-horror game: always unsafe, and always watching for the next threat.

Psychologist Stanley Rachman, an expert in obsessive-compulsive behaviors and anxiety disorders, defines contamination as "an intense and persisting feeling of having been polluted, dirtied,

THE UNCONTROLLABLE MUTINEER: FUNGI AND FEAR IN THE LAST OF US

or endangered as a result of contact, direct or indirect, with an item/place/person perceived to be soiled, impure, dirty, infectious, or harmful." He adds that people who believe they are vulnerable to contamination are "persistently anxious, excessively vigilant and highly avoidant" – much like the protagonists in *The Last of Us*, hiding behind walls, weaving through sewers and tunnels, always on the cusp of succumbing to human or undead foes.

The Last of Us zombies embody many of the "pollutants" that Rachman associates with contamination – putrefying flesh and decaying vegetable matter – with mycelial growths embodying both life and undeath in a hybrid human-fungus body, inviting disgust and avoidance in player and character alike.

The game's tension hinges on the horrid physicality of these undead. We see this first through "runners" – early-stage zombies that could have walked off the set of *28 Days Later*. There are also the more distorted "clickers", with bulbous heads distorted by fungal growth, who can now only detect intruders through a kind of click-based sonar. Then there are "bloaters" and "shamblers", bloated undead creatures packed with pestilence, emitting spores or belching sprays of acid as they come into contact with you, like bursting the stomach of a long-dead animal in a sewer.

In *The Last of Us: Part II*, the hulking Rat King memorably shows the next evolution of the cordyceps virus. This rotting body consists of various, conjoined infected – where blood, pus, flesh and limbs merge into a single monstrosity, a walking plague.

Humans are generally averse to anything seen as rotten, or poisoned, to protect the body from sickness – a natural evolutionary response designed to keep us healthy. But this means the player must push forward through the game while still pulling back from what is deemed unclean. Players are caught in a tense face-off between agency and their own disgust.

 "BILLIONS OF PUPPETS"

HBO's recent TV adaptation of *The Last of Us*, while generally faithful to the original game, takes some liberties to show the context of the wider world pre-cordyceps collapse, and to prime our aversion to the coming fungal outbreak. The first episode opens with an epidemiologist talk show guest, explaining the possible path to a deadly fungal catastrophe in the future:

> *The fungus needs food to live, so it begins to devour its host from within, replacing the ant's brain with its own. But it doesn't let its victim die, no – it keeps its puppet alive. [If this spreads to humans, we're faced with] billions of puppets with poisoned minds, permanently fixed on one unifying goal: to spread the infection to every last human alive.*

Here, poison and control are synonymous – the rot of infected flesh is something that rots our willpower, consuming us and forcing us to consume in turn.

As the academic Amy M. Green says, *The Last of Us* "focuses on the horrors of losing one's mental faculties and control to the infection." From this perspective, a zombie bite is not simply a death sentence, but an assimilation into the group. (i.e. The ant scuttles to its grave to inflict the same fate on its own community.)

This theme recalls the first on-screen zombies in 1932's *White Zombie*, where the undead follow orders in a hypnotic trance. Even the film's original theatrical release poster cites a submissive loss of control: "With these zombie eyes, he rendered her powerless [...] With this zombie grip, he made her perform his every desire."

There are meaningful parallels here between human and zombie control. In *The Last of Us*, the FEDRA totalitarian government, born from the wreckage of the U.S. federal state, is also an extension or analogy of sorts for the cordyceps fungus, a force seeking to control the remaining human population at any cost.

In their essay "Some Kind of Virus: The Zombie as Body and as Trope," critics Webb and Byrnand argue that the thin line between human and zombie is what makes them horrifyingly familiar. They are people just like us, inverted and dangerously close to what we could become: "There is always something 'nearly me' about the monster. This is evident in how easily we are infected with 'zombie-ness': a mere bite from one of them, or a drop of their bodily fluid into my eye, and I too become a zombie."

In an interactive medium like a video game, where player agency is a crucial element to the narrative, this is doubly terrifying. We are continually threatened by the idea that we will lose agency removed from us, and see our bodies and minds bent towards the goal of the fungal other. The power of *The Last of Us* narrative's final moments – where Joel mercilessly guns down an entire medical facility full of resistance fighters and scientists, in order to keep Ellie alive – lies in the complete agency he has in that moment. The ending shows the fulfilment of his will, and the evasion of cordyceps contamination and control, could mean destruction for mankind, ending the hope for a cure the player has spent the whole game working toward.

In ancient Greece, carriers of disease would often be sacrificed outside the city's bounds, in the hope of appealing for an end to the epidemic. *The Last of Us* reverses this impulse, with Joel rescuing the carrier (Ellie) and laying waste to the city instead, inadvertently doing the dirty work of the fungus on its behalf.

Pop culture critic Dahlia Schweitzer, writing on the evolution of the zombie trope over the past century, points out how disaster movies have gradually moved from external threats to internal ones, mirroring a growing awareness of viral outbreaks and biological science among the populace. She writes:

> *Starting in the 1990s, the outbreak narrative turned these metaphors literal. The threat was no longer from the outside but the inside, not so much a threat to the body from aliens or monsters or Bolsheviks, but the body literally acting as a threat. Significantly enlarged microscopic views of deadly germs attacking bodily cells became visualizations for this new kind of invasion. Outer space was replaced with inner space, the body 'simultaneously an uncontrollable mutineer and vulnerable victim.'*

As anxieties around viral outbreaks and pandemics increased, so did their depiction in popular media. This shift also reflects our understanding of danger as something external to something inside of us, where our own body could be victim and enemy both – fighting against both an infection and our will at the same time.

In that kind of world, it is no surprise that the characters in *The Last of Us* are terrified of losing not only their lives, but their sense of control. The back-and-forth revenge narrative of Ellie and Abby in *The Last of Us: Part II* is a natural extension of this fear, as traumatized survivors seek to end the life of whoever killed those closest to them, desperately trying to regain control from the people who took it from them. Green makes this point:

> *The game presents a world of limited control and agency gained through small choices, some of them to terrible ends. For example, after Joel's smuggling partner and possible lover, Tess, is infected, she chooses to end her life in a shoot-out with government forces, thereby buying Joel and Ellie time for an escape. Tess's demise is certain, the method within her control.*

We see this kind of choice made time again – including in *The Last of Us: Part II*, where both Ellie and the playable Abby are caught in a loop of revenge around each other's actions. They gun down the killer of their father, father figure, or friends, seeking to reassert control over those they perceive took it from them.

These characters will do anything to avoid losing their agency — defying imminent infection, a calm home life, or even the last hope of a cure — to hold on to that feeling of control. They push back the rot that is now walking the land, overcoming their fellow humans, and gnawing at the edges of their souls.

As players, we find ourselves in control of that "uncontrollable mutineer," trying to keep Joel, Ellie, or Abby alive, but unable to change their path — or to protect them, ultimately, from themselves.

About the Author

HENRY ST LEGER (he/they) is a journalist, critic, and storyteller based in London, UK. Their writing on games has featured in *The Times*, *Edge*, *GamesRadar* and *Dicebreaker*; they also contributed the introduction to Geek Therapeutics' *The Psychology of Elden Ring*.

References

BBC Studios. (2008, November 3). Cordyceps: attack of the killer fungi – Planet Earth Attenborough BBC wildlife [Video]. YouTube. https://www.youtube.com/watch?v=XuKjBIBBAL8

Citroner, G. (2020, June 10). 'Nearly 20% of People Have Used Bleach on Food due to COVID-19'. Healthline. https://www.healthline.com/health-news/please-do-not-put-bleach-on-food-to-avoid-covid-19

Cooke, J. (2009). Legacies of Plague in Literature, Theory and Film. Palgrave Macmillan.

Druckmann, N. (Writer, Executive Producer) and Mazin, C. (Writer, Executive Producer). (2023). 'When You're Lost in the Darkness' (Season 1, Episode 1) [TV series episode]. In N. Druckmann (Executive Producer), *The Last of Us*. Max. https://www.max.com

Green, A. M. (2016) 'The reconstruction of morality and the evolution of naturalism in The Last of Us'. Games and Culture, 11(7-8), 745-763. https://doi.org/10.1177/1555412015579489

Kainz, K., Bauer, M.A., Madeo, F., & Carmona-Gutierrez, D., 'Fungal infections in humans:

the silent crisis'. Microbial Cell 7(6), 143-145. https://doi.org/10.15698/mic2020.06.718

Lu, J. (2019, April 18). 'How a parasitic fungus turns ants into zombies'. National Geographic. https://www.nationalgeographic.com/animals/article/cordyceps-zombie-fungus-takes-over-ants?loggedin=true&rnd=1696238332068

Rachman, S. (2006). Fear of Contamination: Assessment and Treatment. Oxford University Press.

Roberts, D. (2023, April 5). 'Picking mushrooms can go horribly wrong. Here's what can happen, according to a toxicologist'. The Conversation. https://theconversation.com/picking-mushrooms-can-go-horribly-wrong-heres-what-can-happen-according-to-a-toxicologist-201381

Schweitzer, D. (2018). Going Viral: Zombies, Viruses, and the End of the World. Rutgers University Press.

Seebacher, C. (1996). 'Mycophobia – a new disease?' Mycoses 39. (Suppl 1):30–32. https://doi.org/10.1111/j.1439-0507.1996.tb00500.x

Takahashi, D. (2013, August 6). 'What inspired The Last Of Us'. VentureBeat. https://venturebeat.com/games/the-last-of-us-creators-inspirations/

Webb, J., & Byrnard, S. (2008). Some Kind of Virus: The Zombie as Body and as Trope, *Body & Society*, 14(2), 83-98. https://doi.org/10.1177/1357034X08090699

LOOK FOR THE LIGHT: SURVIVING GRIEF IN A WORLD GONE DARK

DANIEL KAUFMANN

"It Was Either Him Or Me." —Joel

 INTRODUCTION

In the desolate landscape of *The Last of Us*, we find more than just a story of survival; we witness the profound psychological journey of its protagonists, Joel and Ellie. As they navigate a world ravaged by loss, their evolving relationship becomes a powerful testament to the human capacity to endure and find meaning in the face of overwhelming grief. The game expertly intertwines the strained action and emotional narrative, creating an opportunity to develop insight into some of the most difficult human experiences imaginable in fiction.

Joel, haunted by the traumatic loss of his daughter, initially meets Ellie as just another delivery, and being less of a human and more an obligation. Through their shared experiences, Joel's grief finds a path towards healing. Ellie, on the other hand, born into a world already broken, demonstrates resilience and a curiosity for life that contrasts the desolation around her. Their companionship illustrates the profound impact of relational bonds in mitigating the pain of bereavement. The gritty reality of *The Last of Us* offers no simple cure for grief, but rather portrays the arduous process of moving forward, one day at a time.

Joel and Ellie's trust in one another is unlikely from the onset. However, it is built up by repeatedly working together to survive in places where either of them may have otherwise perished. The support they provide to one another, often amidst harrowing circumstances, showcases the therapeutic power of human connection. It is in their silent exchanges, shared struggles, and protection of one another that both characters find the courage to face their pasts and embrace the present. This chapter explores the grief coursing through the depths of Joel and Ellie's psyches — how their bond serves as their beacon, guiding them through the darkness of their internal (and the external) world. In the wake of society's collapse, it is the light of their shared humanity that gives them — and the players controlling them — a deeper understanding of hope.

This chapter draws upon the visceral experiences of Joel and Ellie to illustrate the complex journey through trauma and the potential for healing in our own lives. As players guide these characters through challenges, they encounter scenarios that can encourage reflection on personal grief and recovery methods. For instance, Joel's gradual acceptance of his vulnerability in the company of Ellie parallels the way we, too, can cautiously open up to others as a step towards healing. Ellie's encounters with loss, and her resolve to find purpose, echo the importance of seeking meaning and growth amidst our own adversities. Through this lens, *The Last of Us* serves not only as a narrative of surviving the aftermath of catastrophe, but also as a medium for understanding the multifaceted nature of grief. The game mirrors the stages of denial, anger, bargaining, depression, and acceptance. They serve as not just narrative tools for a game, but as waypoints in the emotional odyssey of trauma resolution, inspiring players to consider their paths to resilience in the real world.

SURVIVING TRAUMA: PROFILES FOR JOEL AND ELLIE

Joel Miller serves as the main playable character for the first entry in *The Last of Us*. His disposition at the start of the game is emblematic of a man internally shattered by the cruel touch of fate — embittered, closed-off, and guarded. Clinical analysis might suggest that he exhibits signs consistent with complex trauma and profound grief, residing in a state of emotional paralysis sustained over the twenty years since the loss of his daughter, Sarah. Joel's survivor's guilt has not only hardened him to the dangers of the postapocalyptic world, but has also hardened barriers around his heart. His interactions are purely transactional, marked by a stark absence of warmth or affinity — an emotional armory erected to avoid the agony of further loss. Joel's once vibrant paternal instincts are buried beneath layers of coping mechanisms, leading to an existence steeped in cynicism and resignation, as he confronts the necessity of survival while the shadow of his trauma lurks in the background.

The primary mission of *The Last of Us* is for Joel to escort the one living immune human across the country to a medical facility guarded by a militant group known as the Fireflies. This girl, Ellie, goes in the eyes of the player from being a mission objective to the heartbeat of the entire game. Ellie's psychological profile contrasts starkly with Joel's at the beginning of *The Last of Us*. Born into a world blighted by the cordyceps outbreak, she adapts with a kind of posttraumatic growth, a phenomenon offering a glimpse into how adversity can be a spark for developing strength, wisdom, and resilience. Unlike Joel, her traumas are not from a world that was lost, but from the harsh realities of the one she has always known.

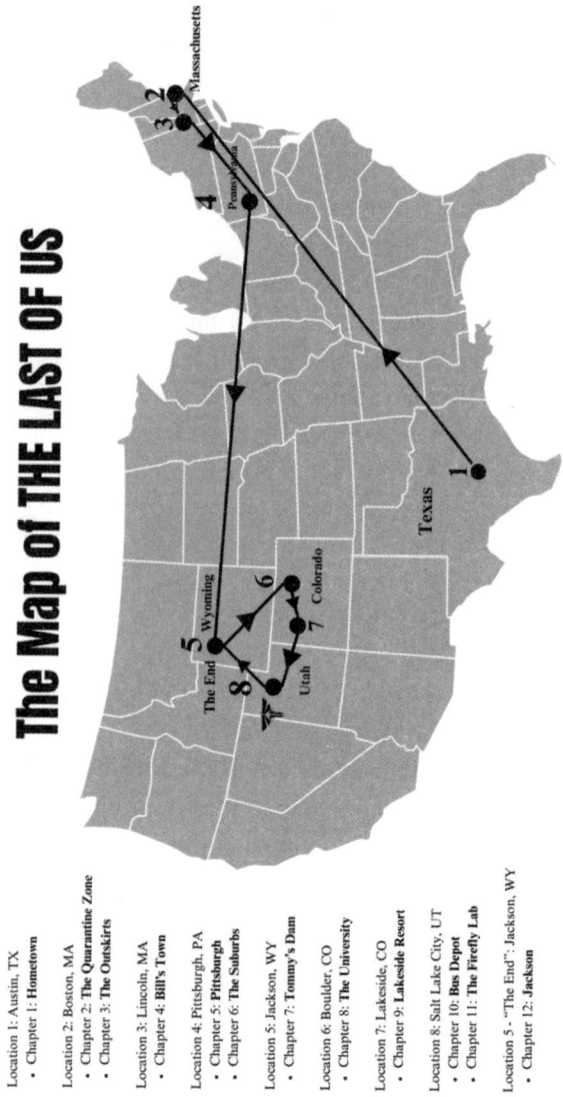

Figure 1. United States Map with the Path of Joel and Ellie in The Last of Us

The *Left Behind* expansion pack to the original game delves even deeper into Ellie's past, revealing the poignant story of her relationship with her best friend Riley. The joy and normalcy this bond brings into Ellie's life is cut tragically short, teaching her the pain of loss firsthand. Although both are bitten, Riley becomes infected and Ellie does not, with the game heavily implying Ellie also had to end the undead form of Riley as she moved beyond the tragedy inside the Boston mall.

From this hardship, Ellie matures beyond her years, understanding that although relationships can end in heartache, they are crucial for providing emotional sustenance in times of desolation. Her remarkable defiance against a world set to the tune of despair is the psychological armor that prepares her to face the perils ahead and makes her a beacon of light in the narrative. The call to adventure in *The Last of Us* is Ellie's to answer, with Joel serving more as a vehicle to fulfilling the grand purpose. Calling on concepts from Viktor Frankl in *Man's Search for Meaning*, "Those who have a 'why' to live, can bear with almost any 'how.'" The "why" is understood most completely by Ellie, with the "how" relying on Joel.

Their histories are not only foundational for later character growth, but also a stark reminder of how fictional stories allow for engagement with complex emotional experiences. Players find healing through a masterful mix of escapism and close identification with characters as the player guides them through the narrative.

 STAGES OF GRIEF & LOSS:
THE PARALLEL TIMELINE

Joel and Ellie's tumultuous journey in *The Last of Us* can be seen as a grim navigation through grief, mirroring the Kubler-Ross model of the five stages of grief. Ellie's situational optimism and Joel's gruff pragmatism start at odds, reflecting their past hardships and the lingering denials they survive.

As the player, we witness both characters go through the immediate shock of realizing their life as they know it is over. After Joel tries in vain to carry his daughter to safety, the checkpoint soldier guns them down on orders from the higher-ups to contain the outbreak at all costs. Once he realizes he is fine and Sarah is not, Joel crawls over and pleads with her all the way through her last breath. As if he can bargain with fate, Joel repeats "Please, please don't do this," as if death can be turned back. In a show of imagery, his watch, the birthday gift he had received hours earlier from Sarah, is damaged. It freezes Joel in the moment where he lost his daughter and the anchor that connected him to his humanity.

Ellie experiences a similar rush from shock to denial to understanding her new reality. Riley dies from the infection, and Ellie does not. Her rage accomplishes nothing, and her despair does even less. Instead, she becomes the chosen one of the story. Ellie, on a conscious level, wanted to die with her friend, but continues to live due to an immunity nobody understands.

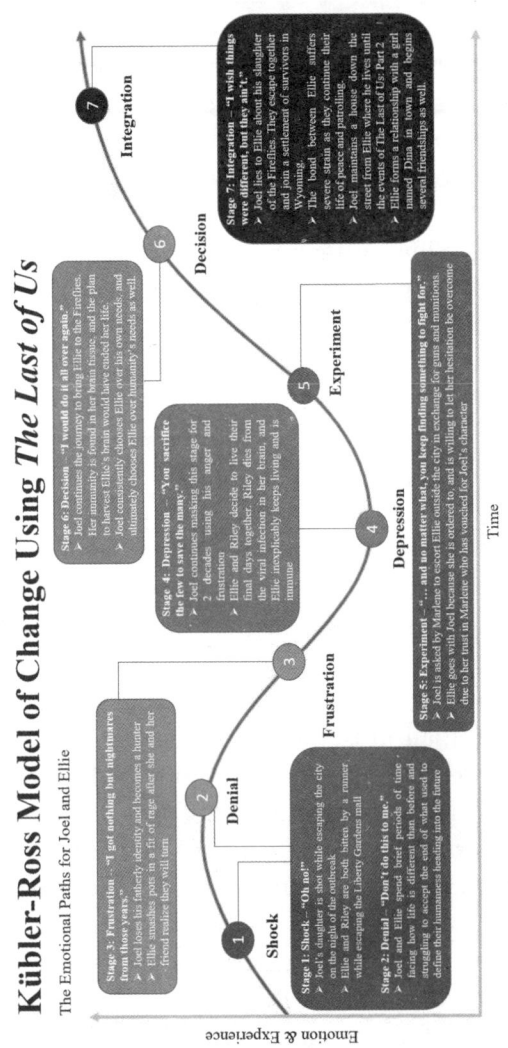

Figure 2. *The Kübler-Ross Model Presented Through* The Last of Us*

- Originally created for use in *The Gamer's Journey* (Kaufmann, 2024) from Leyline Publishing.

Now that both Joel and Ellie are broken beyond their original identities, they can find ways across the entire first entry in the series to heal in their own ways together. Since Joel was a father in his past life, the vow to deliver Ellie to the Fireflies forces him to finally move past his state of avoidance, or die with a bitter futility. In fact, we see him in moments resist this parallel, violently rejecting Ellie's attempts to learn about Sarah across the entire course of the game until the very end. As the representative of hope for humanity, Ellie's future finds a purpose. This allows any hardship to feel like an obstacle worth enduring.

Pushed together as if by fate, Joel and Ellie now have a mission that forces them to grow beyond the suffering state they were in when they first met. While the world they knew is gone, the journey they intend to go on throughout the game holds the best last hope for the living. As they encounter the infected and witness the brutality of other survivors, memories of their past anger resurface, often manifesting in their most vulnerable moments with each other.

We observe bargaining in their fleeting hopes and deals with other characters, all in the pursuit of carrying on. Whether it is Tess trading ration cards for information or Bill settling a debt, leveraging transactional relationships provides everyone with a place in the hierarchy of *The Last of Us*. Trading favors also mirrors each character's choices along their path toward their fate. Although this bargaining does not work, and it aids the character in accepting their surroundings and how to make the most of it.

Accepting what is and what cannot be changed is the most reliable path to an enlightened interpretation of *The Last of Us* as well. The oppressive atmosphere of the game is marked by heartache and desolation. In this way, the world tells the story of the depression stage. Any time we visit a manmade city, we walk through areas that were once functional, now laying in ruin.

Nature, however, is in a much better state, angling to take back the cities and blend this land back in with the growing world of life that is free of human dependency.

This traumatic ruin is a constant companion to both main characters as well. Joel experiences nightmares on a daily basis, awakening to the grim reality that he is still alive despite his losses. Ellie struggles to understand the world that was lost, and at times feels completely alone, waiting to be abandoned eventually by everyone she grows to rely on. These emotional stances oscillate between acceptance and struggle depending on how dire each stop is on their mission. However, in the final act of the game, acceptance becomes transcendent, culminating in an absolute trust as both Joel and Ellie come to believe their mission will be completed successfully together. Ellie even comments on "when we have a cure," or "I can't wait to not have to worry about...," in casual conversation in Salt Lake City. Through their shared experiences, they have been able to confront their past and begin to envision the possibilities in their future.

For players immersed in *The Last of Us*, engaging with Joel and Ellie's emotional odyssey offers a unique form of catharsis, as their trek through the stages of grief parallels real-world healing processes. As players guide the characters through their despair, bargaining, and acceptance, they too may reflect on their own losses, using the gameplay as a medium to process and understand their emotions. Just as Ellie transforms her pain into a source of resilience, players might find solace in their journey, embracing the game's narrative as an outlet for grief and a stepping stone towards personal healing. The interactive nature of the game allows for an intimate connection with the characters' struggles, providing a space for players to confront and perhaps find comfort in their own, often complex, paths to recovery.

 TRUST, RELATIONSHIPS, & PURPOSE

The Last of Us shows us a comprehensive example of how the stages of grief are not a linear experience. Instead, they are a journey that Joel and Ellie push through, experiencing stages repeatedly in an individual way that becomes more successful as they develop their bond together. Each leg of the journey provides the duo with more information, and a new hint of where they might find the Fireflies next. At first, Joel's mandate to Ellie is akin to an authoritarian relationship, illustrated by phrases such as "When I speak, you listen." Being the child in this dynamic, Ellie accepts this, but occasionally pushes back on certain things like needed a gun and being able to contribute. Joel rejects these pleas at first, but through the gameplay constructions of needing Ellie to knock down ladders or unlock doors by boosting to the higher level of ground, Joel (and the player) starts to notice that they are stronger together than they would be individually. While the Boston mission forms the initial foundation for Joel and Ellie's bond of trust, this version of their connection reflects a different style of relationship than what will become as they leave Massachusetts and move into the exploratory phases of their travels.

As Ellie's journey with Joel progresses beyond Boston, her interactions with other survivors reveal more nuances to her personality. For example, when confronting Bill, a survivalist with a cantankerous demeanor, Ellie's tone shifts remarkably from the deference she often maintains with Joel. Her brashness in yelling at Bill stems not just from his abrasive nature, but it also highlights Ellie's increasing assertiveness and willingness to challenge authority when she perceives injustice or folly. This behavior underscores the evolution of her character from a guarded orphan into a confident and staunch survivor, unafraid to speak her mind and stand her ground, even in the face of potential danger or conflict. While Bill does not have a parental stance in his personality like Joel does, Ellie rejects his gruff demeanor, as if she believes people can be at least nice and that first impressions are difficult to rewrite. There is no relationship there, leaving Joel in a tougher spot as he bargains with Bill to get them a car.

The level of trust the player forms with Ellie is reflected in the action and banter of each chapter. This is a common dynamic in people who have experienced rejection and frequent loss, as Ellie has her whole life. Her mother gave birth to her, but died from the cordyceps infection or related decisions not to turn. Marlene, the leader of the Fireflies, turns her care over to Joel and Tess, due to safety concerns in Boston. This makes the rift Ellie feels even more devastating when Joel reveals that, for almost the entire time, he had planned on dropping the responsibility on Tommy to take her all the way to Fireflies. When they reach Wyoming, Joel's drastic shift is jarring even for the player, as all previous comments seemed like Tommy was another stop for gathering information to decide on a clearer path. When Ellie realizes even Joel will abandon her, she flees, making her choice in a fight-or-flight response that risks the safety of everyone invested in the current journey.

Ellie's confrontation with rejection surfaces poignantly when Joel, grappling with the weight of his past and the responsibility of the mission, decides to pass her off to his brother, Tommy. In this moment, she faces not only the sting of abandonment but also a challenge to her developing sense of purpose. Despite her tough exterior, this act threatens to unravel the trust and camaraderie she has built with Joel. Ellie's hurt is palpable; she feels discarded, a reminder of the many times she has been let down before. This pivotal scene lays bare the emotional underpinnings of their relationship and magnifies the depth of Ellie's reliance on Joel, not just for survival, but for the connection she desperately needs in the desolate world they navigate together.

Joel changes his mind after surviving an ambush in the ranch near Tommy's Dam. This growth in moral decision making shows Joel is willing to believe in doing good even if it means some personal sacrifice. As the two of them decide to make their way to University of Eastern Colorado, they are faced with a monumental challenge: Joel is impaled in a fall and is dying. This causes possibly the most dramatic change to gameplay from the beginning to end of the game; the player must now find a way to survive as Ellie.

The gameplay dynamics undergo a startling transformation when players assume control of Ellie. Where Joel represents the hardened survivor accustomed to the brutal world of *The Last of Us*, Ellie's perspective as a young girl thrust into the protagonist's role subverts expectations. This narrative pivot underscores the game's exploration of vulnerability and strength in youth. As Ellie, players must navigate a world that is exceptionally hostile towards a child. For example, certain scenes include moments where being caught off guard result in instant death for Ellie, while similar moments with Joel may contain only an escape mini-game. Going further, Ellie faces additional threats of her autonomy being taken from her, risking evils from David that she did not with Joel. Even so, Ellie's resilience shines as players guide her through each trial, her youthful determination transforming what at first appears as a liability into an unleashed resilience to stab and fight her way through overwhelming odds coming from the cannibal group.

Going back to taking risks for the good of the group, Ellie rises to the responsibility of finding food and medicine for Joel as he battles for his life in a Colorado basement. This world is now built on trauma, and so any group struggling to survive must overcome these societal contexts. The closeness Ellie feels to Joel after he changes his mind leads to healing in the relationship, while her fear of being alone prompts her to battle through anything until she finds herself unable to continue. Joel comes to, and finds her in a rage cutting through her would-be abuser. In this moment, we see an example of how bonds with trusted others bring us back from defeat in the face of systemic trauma. By relying on each other at their weakest moments, both Joel and Ellie show us a powerful gaming example of posttraumatic growth.

STRONGER TOGETHER: THE ETHOS OF THE FIREFLIES

In the landscape of *The Last of Us*, the Fireflies represent a group of resistance fighters who operate in opposition to the established military control of quarantine zones, known as the Federal Disaster Response Agency (FEDRA). The Fireflies challenge the heavy-handed rule of FEDRA, which has been criticized for its oppressive tactics and rigid control in the wake of the cordyceps fungal outbreak. The Fireflies advocate for the return of all governmental power to the people and actively seek a vaccine to the infection, symbolizing hope for a cure and a restoration of societal freedom.

In this grim world, the military's primary focus is on maintaining order within the quarantine zones, often at the expense of individual freedoms and human dignity. Their authoritative grip includes rationing of resources, mandatory curfews, and brutal responses to dissent. The clash between the Fireflies and the military is ideological; a fight between authoritarian stability and a desire for democratic rejuvenation amidst the apocalypse. The unrest is fueled by the military's failures to protect the population and the Fireflies' insistence on finding hope in desperate times, creating a perpetual struggle for power and control within this chaotic new world order.

The concept of meaningful reconstruction during grief is put into sharp focus with the Fireflies in *The Last of Us*. As survivors coping with loss on an unimaginable scale, the Fireflies seek to find purpose amidst the ruins of society by channeling their grief into the fight for a cure, and in doing so, rebuilding a sense of meaning in their lives. In the wake of devastating loss, the human need to make sense of suffering often manifests through the pursuit of noble causes, allowing individuals to reclaim agency in a world that has been irrevocably altered. The Fireflies embody this psychological process by using their collective mourning not as an anchor that weighs them down, but as a catalyst for change and hope. Through their efforts to synthesize a vaccine, they not only strive to prevent further loss, but also to reconstruct a narrative of resilience and fortitude, channeling their grief into a testament of human will and persistence.

The Fireflies' ethos of "finding the light" amidst the darkness is emblematic of their resilience and determination to rebuild what was lost. This sentiment resonates powerfully with the journey of Joel and Ellie — their mutual reliance and evolving bond make them a formidable team in the treacherous world of *The Last of Us*. Just as the Fireflies gain strength from their shared vision and collective action, Joel and Ellie's partnership is enriched and strengthened by their experiences and hardships.

Joel's protectiveness and survival skills paired with Ellie's tenacity and resourcefulness illustrate the concept that they are indeed stronger together. Joel and Ellie's story is a testament to the fact that even in the darkest of places, finding someone to trust can ignite a light powerful enough to guide the way. Through their symbiotic relationship, they embody the Fireflies' creed, demonstrating that even in a world dominated by despair and violence, unity and shared purpose can spawn a glimmer of hope and potential for change.

TRADING THE WORLD FOR A CHANCE AT HAPPINESS

Upon finally reaching the Fireflies, Joel and Ellie are confronted with a devastating moral dilemma — the potential cure for humanity resides within Ellie, but extracting it would result in her death. This revelation rocks Joel to his core, as the bond he has formed with Ellie has grown to mirror that of a father to a daughter, rendering the decision inconceivable to him. Ellie, ever the brave soul, understands the gravity of the situation, yet is willing to make the ultimate sacrifice for the greater good. Her selfless courage highlights the bleakness and beauty of the human condition; a willingness to forfeit one's own life in hope of giving others a chance to reclaim theirs. This harrowing choice encapsulates the game's deeply emotional exploration of love, sacrifice, and the complex nature of hope.

Even though we never see Ellie conscious in the Firefly facility at Saint Mary's Hospital, it appears from Joel's perspective that she either agreed to receive assistance, or was resuscitated from drowning but not brought back to consciousness before her pending surgery. Had this surgery gone through, Ellie's memory would certainly have ascended to heroic status for some sects of the surviving world. It also would have validated the struggle players pushed Joel and Ellie through across the entire game.

Unfortunately, Joel cannot accept this sacrifice.

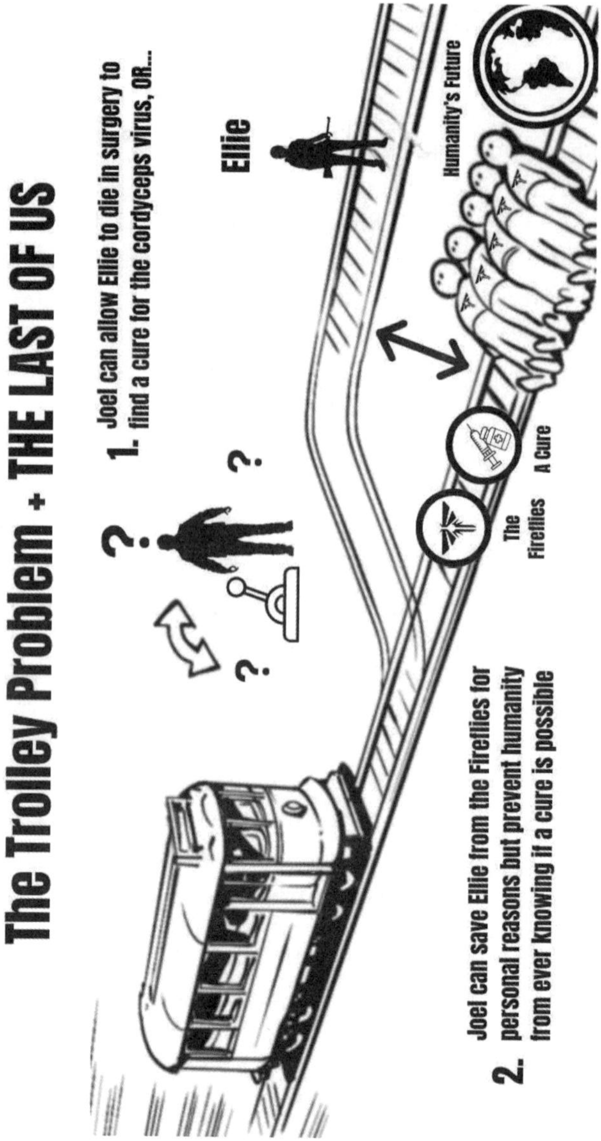

Figure 3. Joel's Decision as The Trolley Problem

Joel's unwillingness to lose Ellie and see her sacrificed is deeply rooted in his personal trauma and loss. Having suffered the pain of losing his own daughter at the onset of the outbreak, Joel finds a second chance at paternal love with Ellie. This rekindled connection revives Joel's protective instincts and fills a void that had been hollow for years. Ellie becomes the personification of redemption and survival for Joel, symbolizing a life tethered to hope rather than shadowed by grief. In her, he sees the potential for healing, for meaningful connection, and for a future — even if it is not the altruistic future the world hopes for. As such, the prospect of losing another daughter-like figure is unthinkable for Joel; it threatens to shatter his world and plunge him back into sorrow. His choice reflects the complex and often paradoxical nature of human emotions. As a worldwide analogy of the trolley problem, in which a person must decide to save only one person and let a group perish, or go the other way and sacrifice the entire group to save a specific person, Joel allows his personal attachment to eclipse the collective need. As a climactic decision to the harrowing experience of *The Last of Us*, the narrative shows its audience a relatable example showcasing the character conflicts that arise due to love and attachment challenging the importance of sacrifice in service to the greater good.

Joel's decision unveils a moral dilemma ripe for reflection: to what extent should individual sacrifice be made in service of the greater good? This philosophical question asks to meditate on the balance between personal anguish and societal benefit. As readers, we must confront the uncomfortable question: would we, in Joel's shoes, prioritize the lives of the many over the life of one beloved person? The answer reveals much about our values, exposing the deep-seated tension between the rationality of utilitarianism and the raw potency of personal bonds. In considering the willingness to sacrifice for a perceived universal benefit, we are forced to grapple with the limits of our altruism and the price of humanity's salvation.

CONCLUSION: THE VALUE OF LIFE

By the time we reach the resolution of this first entry in *The Last of Us* story, the complex tapestry of human emotion and moral dilemmas is laid bare by reviewing the processes of grief and loss in a world struggling to survive. By tracing Joel and Ellie's perilous journey through the dystopian landscape, we see how their bond deepens into a relationship akin to that of a father and daughter, with each character's development mirroring the game's exploration of sacrifice and survival. As witnesses to the heart-wrenching choice at the game's climax — a testament to the game's narrative strength — we are tasked with reflecting on philosophical questions involving what makes something right, and what slight shifts can cause something that feels right to become wrong. What choices would you have made in Joel's place? Do these in-game decisions correlate with your real-world moral compass, and what might this suggest about the power of interactive storytelling to influence our perceptions of right and wrong?

As we ponder the ethical dimensions of Joel's final decision, we can all argue what we think we would have done and why. This debate reveals how complex the human condition truly is. In the end, none of us will ever truly know what we would have done if we had the same exact history as Joel. One thing we do know is what lessons we have learned in the way of thoughts, feelings, and memories from our time shooting, hiding, and stealthing our way across the country — hoping in some small way to find hope for humanity to find its light in a world long since going dark.

About the Author

DR. DANIEL KAUFMANN is an Associate Professor at Grand Canyon University and has served in multiple roles related to program development for gaming and geek therapy training for a variety of clinical settings. His research on the psychology of player types has been presented internationally and continues to evolve with each new world players can inhabit across PCs and consoles. Dr. Kaufmann's publications cover the areas of video games, personality theory, online education, and counselor development. He offers supervision to an international list of clinicians to help bridge the gap in learning about technological impact on society and specific insights related to effectively using games as a positive addition to treatment for clients looking to their gaming activities for inspiration.

Dr. Kaufmann is a fearless advocate for the positive elements of video games, and credits them with many of the thought processes that have proved critical in helping him overcome professional and personal journeys in life. As a result, Dr. Kaufmann became more involved in the Geek Therapeutics community in 2020 as a presenter for online training, content writer, and author. This directly led to using his passion for psychology and mythology to lead him to writing this book, The Gamer's Journey.

References

Avis, K.A., Stroebe, M.S., & Schut, H.A. (2021). Stages of Grief Portrayed on the Internet: A Systematic Analysis and Critical Appraisal. *Frontiers in Psychology, 12.*

Bolden, L. A. (2007). A review of on grief and grieving: Finding the meaning of grief through the five stages of loss. *Counseling and Values, 51*(3), 235-238.

Bugen, L.A. (1977). Human grief: a model for prediction and intervention. *The American journal of orthopsychiatry, 47 2*, 196-206.

Davis, C. G. (2001). The tormented and the transformed: Understanding responses to loss and trauma. In R. A. Neimeyer (Ed.), *Meaning reconstruction & the experience of loss* (pp. 137–155). American Psychological Association.

Frankl, V. (1959). *Man's Search For Meaning.* Beacon Press.

Gomes, R.R. (2020). Trauma, empathy and complicity in The Last of Us Part II: playing as enemy characters. *Antares: letras e humanidades.*

Harrer, S. (2013). From Losing to Loss: Exploring the Expressive Capacities of Videogames Beyond Death as Failure. *Culture Unbound: Journal of Current Cultural Research, 5,* 607-620.

Holland, J.M., & Neimeyer, R.A. (2010). An Examination of Stage Theory of Grief among Individuals Bereaved by Natural and Violent Causes: A Meaning-Oriented Contribution. *OMEGA — Journal of Death and Dying, 61,* 103 - 120.

Kaufmann, D. A. (2024). *The Gamer's Journey.* Leyline Publishing.

Kübler-Ross, E., & Kessler, D. (2014). *On grief and grieving: Finding the meaning of grief through the five stages of loss*. Simon and Schuster.

López-Zerón, G., & Blow, A.J. (2017). The role of relationships and families in healing from trauma. *Journal of Family Therapy, 39*, 580-597.

Maciejewski, P. K., Zhang, B., Block, S. D., & Prigerson, H. G. (2007). An Empirical Examination of the Stage Theory of Grief. *JAMA, 297*(7), 716-724. https://doi.org/10.1001/jama.297.7.716

McGuire, B.F. (2020). Gaming and Grieving: Digital Games as Means of Confronting and Coping with Death. *The Journal of Religion, Media and Digital Culture, 9*, 326-346.

Neimeyer, R. A. (2001). *Meaning reconstruction & the experience of loss*. American Psychological Association.

Schultz, K., Cattaneo, L.B., Sabina, C., Brunner, L.T., Jackson, S., & Serrata, J.V. (2016). Key roles of community connectedness in healing from trauma. *Psychology of Violence, 6*, 42-48.

A BOND WORTH MORE THAN ALL THE WORLD: THE ROLE OF ADOPTION IN *THE LAST OF US*

AMANDA DUNCAN AND BRYAN DUNCAN

"If I ever were to lose you, I'd surely lose myself" —Joel Miller

CONNECTION THROUGH ADOPTION AS DEPICTED IN *THE LAST OF US*

Family is a concept that has many meanings to society. One such is the concept of 'found family' — when individuals that once had no connection at all suddenly connect on the same levels as biological families. *The Last of Us* offers a beautiful story between a "found family" and how this connection grows and evolves over time. This chapter will specifically explore the role of adoption in found families.

HOW IT ALL BEGAN

The Last of Us is a TV show in the post-apocalyptic/survival/horror genre. The series opens with the world in a state of panic due to a fungus that is plaguing society. As the story unfolds, humans become infected with the fungus and transform into a hive mind zombie.

There is only one human immune to the fungus — Ellie, a 14-year-old orphaned girl. Ellie is under the protection of a freedom fighter leader, Marlene, who discovers Ellie's immunity and believes she holds the key to a cure. Marlene recruits Joel, a survivor hardened by the tragic death of his daughter, to transport Ellie to a medical facility. Joel has become desensitized and cynical, caring only about survival at any cost. He therefore takes risky, illicit assignments outside the safety of the quarantine zone for profit. Joel and Ellie meet and begin the journey of their lives intertwining together. The relationship between Joel and Ellie in *The Last of Us* is both layered and complex. When they first meet, Joel is he thinks of Ellie as nothing more than cargo. He attaches no emotion to her, only caring about the prize at the end. He has no intention of viewing Ellie as the vulnerable young woman she is. To see her as anything else would go against everything he has stood for since the death of his daughter.

Joel and Ellie have a combative relationship in the beginning as they begin their journey. Joel treats Ellie as an object without a voice, and in return she is antagonistic towards Joel.. Joel's romantic and business partner, Tess, serves as a buffer between Joel and Ellie. She offers a softer approach with Ellie and recognizes her humanity and individuality, which helps Ellie's relationship with Joel to evolve. Unfortunately, Tess sacrifices herself after being infected early in their journey, and Ellie and Joel are left to deal with each other's personalities and interaction styles on their own. Ellie begins to recognize her dependence on Joel for survival. Joel responds to Ellie's newfound openness to learning and becomes a mentor to her. This new mindset has moved the relationship between the two into a teacher/learner scenario for a short period of time.

EVOLVING RELATIONSHIP

In the next phase of their relationship, Joel and Ellie provide comfort and care for each other as situations arise. Alone in their journey together, they learn to rely on one another. Ellie cares for a wounded Joel and helps nurse him back to health. Without Ellie, Joel might not survive the trauma resulting from his injuries. Joel provides comfort to Ellie as she encounters new horror and loss of life outside of the quarantine zone. Ellie has not experienced these things before, so she is forced to rely on Joel for support. As they take turns in a nurturer role, a new softness develops in their relationship.

Finally, at the climax of the narrative, Joel delivers Ellie to the medical team, completing his mission. Heartbroken, he discovers that to save humanity from the fungal infection, Ellie will have to sacrifice her life. Joel begins to discover that he cares for Ellie as he did his own late daughter, Sarah. His love for Ellie overtakes his logic. Unwilling to sacrifice another daughter to the horrors of this post-apocalyptic world, Joel fights back. He rescues Ellie in a carnage-filled firefight — saving his daughter figure while dooming the world to the zombie plague in the process. Joel's bond to Ellie is worth more to him than saving the world, making this story a very different kind of heroic narrative. What were once priorities have quickly faded away at the thought of losing Ellie. Rewards and completing the job become suddenly irrelevant to Joel.

ADOPTIVE RELATIONSHIPS: THE UNTOUCHABLE CONNECTION

Adoptive relationships are inherently complicated, especially in the beginning. Many begin with great amounts of conflict. Shared experiences can ultimately outweigh this conflict, creating an overall positive experience for both parental figures and the surrogate child or teen. This topic is illustrated in Joel and Ellie's relationship as they go from tense to a more cohesive 'family'" as their shared experiences grow. As Ellie and Joel communicate and share their perspectives with each other, this newfound empathy grows their relationship to new heights. This is consistent with the real-life process by which adolescents' bond with fostering caretakers evolves.

Additionally, found families often create rituals unique to the family. Joel may inadvertently create such rituals while teaching Ellie to survive. These become a part of their relationship and shared dynamic. Another mechanism for building a bond is in offering support to one another, which Joel and Ellie do on several occasions throughout their ordeal. Joel ultimately grows to care for Ellie in a way that has elements of parental care, including risking himself to save and protect her. Those playing parental roles in the lives of children and teens placed in their care tend to report a more cohesive sense of family and family membership when caring behaviors are produced by the adopter and are perceived as such by the adoptee. In *The Last of Us*, Joel does much to provide for Ellie in terms of food, shelter, and protection. Ellie will later provide food, shelter, and ultimately medicine for an incapacitated Joel. Each individual recognizes the effort and risk the other takes to care for the other. This reciprocal interaction serves to reinforce and grow their bond. Thus, the father/daughter relationship buds. Joel and Ellie now rely on each other because of their love for one another.

 BONDING IN ADOPTIVE RELATIONSHIPS

At times it takes a direct strategy to improve bonding in an adoptive relationship. The fostering caretaker must make the child feel as if they belong, giving them a sense of security. This strategy was not really applied by Joel until later in the story; in fact, this strategy seems to be the lowest of his priorities. Another factor attributed to successful bonding is that of structure and guidance. Joel creates that environment inadvertently as he sets structure he sees as protective for himself and Ellie. He guides her in survival techniques and secures their bond through the consistency of his actions and care. Throughout his interactions with Ellie, Joel is consistently himself. Despite several conflicts he proves himself a dependable and predictable presence in her life as they traverse the countryside. Through this development, Ellie begins to trust Joel. He is a stable figure in an unstable world. Ellie has never experienced a bond to as secure or meaningful as she does with Joel.

Adoptive relationships like Joel and Ellie's can vary greatly, depending on personalities, lifestyles, and environments. Overall, it seems that adoptive relationships are positive learning experiences for both parties involved. Studies show that once the adoptive relationship commences, things like parental affection and mentality change. Suddenly, there is someone else in the world they can rely on and that directly contributes to the growth of the relationship. This safety is imperative to the bonding of the relationship. Both sides of the relationship need to feel secure in order to deepen the bond.

 ADOPTIVE VERSUS BIOLOGICAL CONNECTIONS

Families with biological children and foster children often bond simultaneously, with parents and siblings mutually connecting over time. Bonding in adoptive families is facilitated when a familiar role is (or has been) present, and serves as a template to model. In Joel's case, he had a daughter, Sarah, who is killed very early in the story. Joel finds himself slowly moving Ellie into the role of daughter as their travels progress. Joel treats Ellie in much the same way he treated Sarah. Ultimately, he protects Ellie as fiercely as he protected Sarah, and finds himself unable to face any potential loss of Ellie.

On the other side, Ellie has no direct emotional connection to her biological parents. Her mother, Anna, only had time to write Ellie a letter between Ellie's birth and Anna's death about a day later. Ellie's father is not named or mentioned as an integrated part of her life. It is insinuated that he is absent. Instead, Marlene, a friend of Anna's, took on the responsibility of looking after Ellie, though she did not directly provide much care for Ellie and instead placed her with a military school. However, Ellie still looks to Marlene for direction and protection. For example, when Ellie is introduced to Joel and Tess, she wants to stay with Marlene rather than leave with these strangers. Marlene is the closest to a parent figure in her life. Later, as Ellie grows closer to Joel, she treats him with a sense of connection different than how she treats Marlene. Ellie finds a caring and protective parent in Joel like she has never had before, and Joel provides direct care and support for Ellie that not even Marlene could provide. Ellie's once-deep connection with Marlene is replaced by Joel, who plays the role of a father more than anything for Ellie.

 THE CHALLENGES OF ADOPTION

Loss can often fuel a bond. For example, a trauma bond occurs when trauma (an isolated incident, or over a period) drives two people together and solidifies their bond through the shared experience(s). In adoptive relationships, a surrogate parent may feel the of loss of certain parenting experiences, such as birthing the child, sharing certain developmental milestones, and much more. Accepting these losses, and at times the process of projecting and imagining those emotions, moments, and bonds with the adoptive child are helpful. Similarly, the child may have experienced loss and disappointment in previous foster situations. They too may feel the loss of a supportive caretaker at special events, guiding or teaching certain skills or bonding moments. As such, adoptive children may have to cycle through pain and loss while connecting to their new caretaker and gaining new experiences and shared moments. This process of dealing with pain and loss to build a new bond is not automatic. It takes work, cultivation, and maintenance on the part of both the adoptive parent and the adoptive child. Though a difficult process, the end of the journey to bonding makes it all worthwhile.

 BLOSSOMING LOVE

As Joel and Ellie progress in their newfound adoptive relationship, we see the spectacular amounts of work it took to grow their relationship into the state it is in by the close of the first game. Ellie, a piece of cargo to Joel in the beginning, is now seen through the lens of attachment as a daughter figure. Joel, a grieving father, has softened and allowed a person to get close to him and feels genuine affection again. This newfound connection has activated Joel's paternal instincts. His desire to shield her from harm and stress is indicative of his feelings of fatherly love. Ellie, a once closed-off teenager who did not give Joel any bonded feelings, now looks to him as a father figure. Ellie's familial bond is the driving force behind her desire to protect Joel when he is injured. She looks to him for guidance and acquisition of new skills. Though not connected by blood, they are connected by heart. As a father to his child, Joel fiercely protects and cares for Ellie. Ellie lovingly cares for her father as a daughter who is concerned with his well-being.

Parents who adopt face many of the same fears as parents who give birth to their children. Adoptive parents do not experience physical labor as the parents of biological children do, but they experience a different kind of labor — emotional labor. This bond is often more difficult to form with some adoptive experiences, such as with teenagers as in the case of Ellie. Ellie, being a teenager at the time, had already experienced childhood and early adolescence. She is now a young woman learning to be an adult. Ellie and Joel do not share first experiences like Ellie learning to crawl, or saying her first words to Joel. Despite this, they can form a bond as if they had always been together. Their bond proves to be strong enough to overtake the current state they are living in. Joel, once in it for the prize, now loves and protects Ellie — so much so that Joel decides that the world cannot have Ellie, even if it comes at such a great cost.

UNPACKING THE HISTORY OF ELLIE

Some aspects of adoption can greatly impact self-esteem and self-perception of the adopted child. Ellie has a start in the letter from her mother, encouraging her to "make me proud." This message informs Ellie's approach to life from a very early age as the only connection to her biological mother. In fact, Ellie's most prized possessions are the letter from her mother and her mother's switchblade knife. When first paired with Joel and Tess, Ellie, who has been shielded in the safe zone, thinks she can care for herself, but quickly sees she cannot survive without the help of Joel and Tess. After Tess' death, Joel and Ellie are left with only one another. Ellie becomes more and more confident in her abilities.

Though not from the process of adoption itself, Ellie's self-esteem and self-efficacy improve from her relationship with Joel. Ellie grows as a person and survivor by being cared for by Joel, and Ellie recognizes this growth within herself.

 SACRIFICE FOR REWARD

Loving and familial relationships often involve some sort of sacrifice and risk. In *The Last of Us*, Joel risks his life to protect Ellie, and is dramatically wounded at one point in the process. Ellie takes a risk as she goes out on her own to care for Joel while he recovers. For Joel the risk is simply about the task at first — getting the cargo (Ellie) to California. He later does so because he genuinely cares about Ellie and has come to see her as he did his own daughter Sarah at the beginning of the story. Ellie at first is not willing to sacrifice for Joel, but ultimately changes her mind for the safety Joel provides her. When she later she comes to think of him as a fatherly figure, she shares her feelings and risks much to care for him. This is a stark difference from their previous relationship with one another.

Joel eventually discovers that to cure the fungal plague that has almost consumed the planet would require Ellie's vivisection and death. Joel finds himself unable let go of this surrogate daughter to those desperate to stop the plague, like he had lost his biological daughter to a soldier when the outbreak began. He risks his life to extradite her from the facility, killing soldiers and some of the few medically experienced individuals left on the planet to get a sedated Ellie out of the facility. This action would doom the planet to continue to suffer from the plague, risking the life of all other humans on earth. He does not tell her what he did to save her life. In the end, he determines this 'found family' between him and Ellie is a bond worth all the world.

 ADOPTIVE RELATIONSHIPS IN *THE LAST OF US*

Overall, the adoptive relationship can be seen in many undertones between Joel and Ellie. Though Joel never officially adopts Ellie, the relationship is still evident. Their relationship mirrors that of adoptive parent and child relationships in the real world. Love, pain, protection, and caring are all seen in the relationship between the two. The connection was neither easy nor automatic; this bond was forged through shared experiences, loss, loneliness, and connection. It is a beautiful story of two people giving of themselves in ways they never thought possible, and in the end the reward is a powerful connection where each one willing to risk much — if not all — for the other.

Players of the game and viewers of the TV series who are from adoptive, foster, or found families, may see a reflection of themselves in *The Last of Us*. Those with close connections to non-biological caregivers, or with those they have mentored or taken care of, may feel validated by the conflict, strife, and struggle such a bond entails, and identify with the priceless reward this bond can be. There are many who may play the games or see the series who long for such a connection to a mentor or a stronger bond to a parent or child. The bond between Joel and Ellie is so inspirational it may motivate others to reach out and make connections to others. Joel and Ellie take a risk in trusting one another and deliberately growing their relationship. Individuals who desire such a familial connection with others can see the work and risk involved in forging bonds Joel and Ellie took, and similarly take risks themselves in strengthening connections with others. The human bond is a beautiful thing that can develop in the most surprising ways and under unexpected conditions. A strong interpersonal bond is in itself the reward for the risk and work of growing connections and can be so central to an individual's life that they would risk anything to keep it — money, safety, their life, or in Joel's case, all of humanity.

About the Authors

BRYAN C. DUNCAN, PHD is a Licensed Psychologist, Licensed Professional Counselor, Supervisor and Nationally Certified Counselor, the Director of Clinical and Training Services at New Leaf Services and Assistant Training Director of Psychology at John Peter Smith Hospital in Fort Worth, Texas. He is a Certified Geek Therapist, a Certified Therapeutic Game Master, and Certified Problematic Gaming Specialist from Geek Therapeutics. Among his areas of expertise are: cognitive behavioral therapy (CBT), Acceptance and Commitment Therapy (ACT), Dialectical Behavior Therapy (DBT) and cognitive processing therapy (CPT), Prolonged Exposure Therapy (PE), and Trauma Focused CBT (TF-CBT), therapy for traumatic experiences, abuse, post-traumatic stress disorder (PTSD), grief counseling, and health issues (including therapy for adjusting to chronic medical conditions; sleep difficulties; exercise, diet, and medical treatment adherence).

AMANDA L. DUNCAN is a master's student in counseling at Dallas Baptist University. She holds a bachelor's degree from Tarleton State University in Business. Amanda has worked in the mental health field for 15+ years and considers it a passion of hers. She is interested in practicing Acceptance and Commitment Therapy, Dialectical Behavioral Therapy and Narrative therapy. Amanda has future plans to obtain her doctorate in psychology and looks forward to contributing to the field of psychology. Amanda enjoys learning new meditations, sleep stories, and spending time with family and pets.

References

Doubledee, R. R. (2015, May 1). *The Effects of Adoption on Foster Children's Well-Being.* https://www.researchgate.net/publication/309563739_The_Effects_of_Adoption_on_Foster_Children's_Well-Being_A_Systematic_Review

Hallas, D. (2002). A model for successful foster child-foster parent relationships. Journal of Pediatric Health Care 3(16). https://www.sciencedirect.com/science/article/abs/pii/S0891524502647790

Heather L. Storer, Susan E. Barkan, Linnea L. Stenhouse, Caroline Eichenlaub, Anastasia Mallillin, Kevin P. Haggerty, In search of connection: The foster youth and caregiver relationship, Children and Youth Services Review, Volume 42, 2014, Pages 110-117, ISSN 0190-7409, https://doi.org/10.1016/j.childyouth.2014.04.008. (https://www.sciencedirect.com/science/article/pii/S0190740914001583)

Holen, F.V., Cle, A., West, D., Gypen, L., Vanderfaeille, J. (2020, December 1). *Family bonds of foster children. A qualitative research regarding the experience of foster children in long-term foster care.* https://www.sciencedirect.com/science/article/abs/pii/S0190740920320168

Maizen, C. & Druckmann, N., (Writers). (2023). HBO

Nicoleau-Poliard, A., Fox, C. A., & Sealy, D.-A. (2023). Bonding With Adolescents in Foster Care: Perspectives of Foster Parents. Journal of Family Issues, 0(0). https://doi.org/10.1177/0192513X231181362

Passmore, N.L., Fogarty, G.J., Bourke, C.J. and Baker-Evans, S.F. (2005), Parental Bonding and Identity Style as Correlates of Self-Esteem Among Adult Adoptees and Nonadoptees†. Family Relations, 54: 523-534. https://doi.org/10.1111/j.1741-3729.2005.00338.x

Waterman B (2001) Mourning the loss builds the bond: Primal communication between foster, adoptive, or stepmother and child, Journal of Loss and Trauma, 6:4, 277 300, DOI: 10.1080/108114401317087806

ALCOHOL AND RAGS: THE CONSEQUENCES OF VIOLENT AGENCY IN A DIGITAL WORLD

ROY WANG

"Everybody I Have Ever Cared For Has Either Died Or Left Me." —Ellie

The ways in which we interact with the world have become increasingly digital. Between email, remote work, and social media, a significant portion of our day-to-day living is spent with screens, and this has blurred the line between the computerized world and our actual reality. Although the digital sphere affects our lives more and more every day, many people still behave as if they are separate. They find it easier to act more brazenly online and are unafraid to do and say things to others that they would not do in person. Their actions take place online, but their impacts have very real consequences. Timothy Welsh describes this psychological concept as a "mixed reality" in *Mixed Realism*:

> *The virtualities of media are increasingly the way in which we come to know about and interact with the world ... Ours is a mixed reality, in which big and small screens blend virtual environments into everyday life ... the virtual and the actual take on a strange equality.*

Hundreds of thousands of hate comments and videos are posted daily all over the internet, contributing to a cycle of emotional violence that has repeatedly laid the foundations for actual acts of physical brutality. What we do in the virtual matters — because it influences how we conduct ourselves in our lives beyond the screen.

Given this relationship, it is no surprise that many people attempt to blame video games for in-person acts of violence., There is a long and visible history of games that allow players to exercise or experience fictional violence. From the pixelated explosions of colorful alien ships to the gunfire bloodshed of modern first-person shooters, violence is one of the simplest and most understood methods of player agency. Simply put, if you see an enemy, you are expected to kill them. In many game genres — especially action games — the primary means of story progression and character advancement occurs through the violence the player enacts on the obstacles standing between their character and their goal.

This game mechanic and its effects were capture in researcher Tilo Hartmann's model of Moral Disengagement in Violent Video Games. Also known as the MoDViG model, this concept suggests that players are able to enjoy violence in video games was due to the way games morally disengage players from their violent actions. Scholars like Holger Pötzsch furthered this model by introducing the idea of four filters: violence, consequence, character, and conflict. Essentially, filters can be thought of as the unspoken rules of video game violence; rules that dictate who can be hurt, the impacts of violence shown and hidden from the audience, which moral side the player advances, and the absence of nonviolent player actions. These filters explain why reason shelves are lined with games in which the player is a male hero who has no choice but to violently dispatch villainous men or monsters with no long-term psychological impacts.

Pötzsch and other scholars have used the concept of filters and the MoDViG model to question the ability of games like *The Last of Us* to tell emotionally and philosophically meaningful stories without being hypocritically sabotaged by their gameplay. Pötzsch writes:

> In *The Last of Us* *the deployment of generic consequence and violence filters causes an ambitious storyline to enter into an unhappy marriage with conventionalized game mechanics that partly undermines the narrative potentials of the game.*

While Pötzsch is correct that *The Last of Us* lacks any ability to peacefully resolve conflicts with enemies through conversation, this does not mean that the series is unable to offer insightful commentary on the nature of violence and its effects on the parties involved.

What scholars like Pötzsch miss in their analyses is a game's ability to make a statement or critique through the purposeful choice of action game as its medium. Action games are like any other art form in that they offer experiences that teach us about the human condition and change our perspectives on social issues — not in spite of their violent gameplay, but because of it. Naughty Dog deliberately uses the violent medium of the action game as the canvas for their story to better highlight — and then subvert — the typical filters that accompany the genre. In doing so, the games teach the player two important lessons: that, even in a brutally dystopic world, nonviolent actions are just as important and impactful as violent ones, and that the effects of violence hurt all parties involved, even the perpetrators.

Considering we live in a mixed reality where a progressively digital world informs and shapes decisions that affect our physical reality, it is important that we do not write off the nuanced arguments of *The Last of Us* and *The Last of Us: Part II* due to the presence of action game mechanics. These games prove that brutality in video games is a unique tool that can craft learning experiences that ultimately teach us to be less violent people, both on- and off-screen, by showcasing the substantial impact of cooperative, pacifist actions and the double-edged consequences of violent agency.

THE LAST OF US: PART I: VIOLENCE TEACHING NONVIOLENCE

Perfect for Righteous Murder

From the outset, *The Last of Us* plants its feet firmly in the action game genre by establishing a setting where fighting and bloodshed are the main means of power. Having Joel begin the game by killing an infected member of the Coopers (a neighbor) Naughty Dog teaches players that the ability to hurt others is an instrumentally effective method for controlling the world. In the same way a child learns from their parents, the player (in the perspective of Joel's daughter, Sarah) learns early on that violence equals personal agency. Joel cannot protect himself or Sarah without being willing and able to maim and kill.

After that initial act of violence, the game takes the player through the downward spiral of Joel's life as the player watches him and Tommy shoot and run over a zombie to get out of the city, reinforcing the connection between violence and control. This connection is affirmed in the last scene of the introduction, when Joel and Sarah meet a soldier. Joel trusts that the soldier is there to help them, and therefore drops his guard. The soldier then takes advantage of Joel's trust and shoots at them, killing Sarah. Before the soldier can kill Joel, Tommy arrives and shoots the soldier, reasserting control of the scene. Beginning the game with the killing of the Coopers and then ending the introduction with Sarah's death reveals a core tenant of *The Last of Us*: if you are unwilling to do violence, then violence will be done unto you. By establishing a world in which violence is a necessity for survival, Naughty Dog creates a seemingly perfect environment for the player to disengage themselves from their violent actions; a proper setting for the brutal gameplay of the typical action game.

The story continues with a time skip, and a second theme is introduced about the importance of cooperation and scarcity of trust. In the world of *The Last of Us*, trust is a valuable resource and, as we see with Sarah's death, will be heavily punished if given to the wrong person. The player's first mission as Joel deals with a breach of trust as Joel and Tess's inventory of weapons are sold behind their backs. Again, the game follows the predictable patterns of the action genre as the game teaches the player to aim, distract, shoot, and stealth kill to accomplish the goal of finding and punishing the traitor. When entrusts Joel and Tess with Ellie, and when Ellie trusts them with the knowledge that she is immune, the game establishes trust as a resource that allows the player to accomplish more than they could on their own. The story champions cooperation — and, as we see when with Tommy kills the soldier and Tess sacrifices herself, trusting other people is an essential component of survival.

Removing the Violent Veil

The seemingly hypocritical interaction between trust and violence has been criticized by many scholars, like Se Young Kim in his essay "Video Game Violence and the Ethics of Empowerment in *The Last of Us*." He writes:

> *...the inevitability of conflict defines* The Last of Us, *as is the unfortunate case with the vast majority of commercial video games ... survival ultimately amounts to weapons, the ability to use them, and ...the willingness to kill.*

Some scholars and players find it problematic to preach the importance of cooperation in *The Last of Us* while the gameplay consists of brutal mass murder. Joel and Ellie ultimately kill approximately 500 NPCs throughout the course of the game. However, this perspective is so focused on the violence of the action game genre that it fails to consider the other mechanics within the game.

The Last of Us subtly undermines the importance of violent agency with its myriad of puzzle elements. Though there are many violent action sequences in the game, a significant portion of the gameplay is dedicated to finding ways around inanimate obstacles. In their trek across the United States, Joel helps Ellie over walls to let down ladders, carries boards to place across gaps, and keeps doors open with cabinets and furniture. Despite the mundane banal and simple nature of these actions, they are necessary for the player to move forward, just as much as the violent sequences in the game. The duo would not have made it to Salt Lake City if Ellie did not trust Joel to float her across a body of water on a precarious wooden pallet, knowing that she would drown if she fell. By tying story progression to a contrasting combination of both mercilessly homicidal gameplay and cooperative, pacifist environmental puzzles, *The Last of Us* creates a dynamic in which personal agency relies equally on players' violent and nonviolent abilities.

Naughty Dog continues to subvert genre expectations with the tragic story of Henry and Sam. This storyline shows the self-destructive nature of violence by breaking the action game's typical violence and consequence filters. Violence and consequence filters dictate who can be hurt, and which effects of violent actions are actively portrayed to the player. For example, most action games have rules that prevent the harming of child NPCs, and many ignore the short- and long-term effects of violence on the main player character's psyche. The beginning of the game, with Sarah's death and Joel's persistent grief, signals to the player that

The Last of Us is not be afraid to cross the unspoken boundaries within the action game genre.

The player now can hold the possibility in their mind that Henry and Sam may die over the course of the game. However, it is the manner in which they died that the game reveals an argument on the nature of violence. Sam is bitten and turns into a zombie. When Sam attacks Ellie, Henry decides to kill his little brother — and upon realizing the severity of his decision, proceeds to shoot himself. In this scene, Naughty Dog exemplifies that no one escapes the effects of violence. Henry, despite knowing that there is no cure for Sam, becomes understandably overwhelmed by the impact of his act of violence. It did not matter that there was no alternative to killing Sam, nor did it matter that his violence saved Ellie and Joel. Henry becomes a victim of his own actions, completing this self-harm through his suicide. By removing the usual violence and consequence filters with the death of a child and a scene of an active suicide, Naughty Dog makes sure that players explicitly experience the idea that one cannot be unscathed by violence, even the perpetrator. In the chapter right after this incident, players see this claim echoed in a conversation between Joel and Tommy about their actions in the early years of the pandemic:

> Tommy: *I got nothing but nightmares from those years.*
> Joel: *You survived because of me!*
> Tommy: *It wasn't worth it.*

With this last phrase, Tommy summarizes the terrible ramifications violent agency can have on the people who use it, and that even self-preservation may not be worth the consequences. Unlike other actions games that glorify or hide the effects of violence to help the player temporarily suspend their concepts of morality, *The Last of Us* grounds itself firmly outside of the usual filters to demonstrate that violence to others is synonymous with violence to oneself.

Killing the Illusion of Choice

The Last of Us establishes that, even in a world where violence is a necessary component of survival, personal agency can still take many forms, both violent and nonviolent. Using the historically murderous genre of action games, Naughty Dog argues that violent agency is a dangerous path that harms victims and perpetrators alike. This concept sees a dramatic representation in the last scene of the game. After learning that the research for a cure requires Ellie's death, Joel slaughters his way through the Fireflies to stop the surgery. Though the surgeon draws his knife when Joel enters the room, he remains passive. No matter how long the player stands in front of him, the surgeon never attacks Joel, and the only option to advance the story is for the player to kill the surgeon.

In this moment, some players may feel that their agency has been taken away. They have no option to choose a nonviolent path — or even enact a nonfatal wound — as the player's next shot kills the surgeon regardless of where they aim. However, what Naughty Dog reveals in this final scene is that the player does not truly have their agency taken away; they never had it to begin with. Despite the contrast of nonviolent and violent sections of the game, the player is never the one choosing their methods.

Like with most action games, violence is necessary to progress in many sections of *The Last of Us*. Players either ignore or remain unaware of their lack of choice due to the common filters, assumptions, and suspensions that accompany the genre. However, when the character filter breaks, and Joel makes a decision that is wholly selfish, players (especially those that disagreed with Joel's choice) finally see the falsehoods of violence. When the player realizes the irreversible impact their actions, and the heroic facade of the protagonist fades. It becomes clear having violence as the only means of personal agency is a terrible position. In this way,

Naughty Dog uses the action game genre against itself. The typical conflict filter that limits player actions to violence is usually what allows players to disengage from their actions and enjoy the bloodshed — but by creating a scenario in which the player was forced to enact violence, *The Last of Us* suddenly turns the typical action game filters against the players' enjoyment. By requiring the player to pull the trigger and kill the surgeon to progress the story, *The Last of Us* makes the player an emotional victim to their own violent actions, not unlike the way that Henry was victimized by his own act of violence against Sam.

THE LAST OF US: PART TWO: REAL HURT FROM VIRTUAL PEOPLE

A Death in the Family

By subverting the typical filters of the action game genre, *The Last of Us* not only showcases the double-sided blade of violent agency, but also positions the player to experience emotional hurt themselves — proving that acts of digital violence can still affect us in the physical world. We see this sentiment in players' passionate reactions to *The Last of Us: Part II*, specifically the moment when the main player character shifts from Ellie to Abby.

Set five years after the first game, *The Last of Us: Part II* shows Joel and Ellie living in a safe, almost modern encampment fully outfitted with electricity, abundant food, and even simple systems of education, government, and economy. After about an hour of gameplay, the main player character shifts from Ellie to Abby, and the players control Abby as she makes her way down to the settlement to find and kill someone. As Abby, the player braves a snowstorm and multiple hordes of infected, and soon realizes it is

Joel she is hunting. The consequence of the player's actions contribute directly to Joel's death. After Joel's brutal death scene, the player character changes back to Ellie as she works to get revenge on Abby for killing Joel. Halfway through the game, Abby and Ellie meet for the first time since Joel's death, and Abby kills one of Ellie's friends. The game then replays the scene of Joel's death before switching back to Abby as the player character, ensuring that Abby is demonized as much as possible before the swap.

Crying Over Code

We see the importance of the change in player characters both in the strength of the players' reactions and their reasons for the backlash. The Korea Advanced Institute of Science and Technology performed a study in 2021 that recorded a variety of player reactions to the game. Within these interviews, the researchers saw a very divisive split in thoughts about the game's narrative, ranging from "one of the bravest narratives I think I've ever interacted with" to "emotionally abusive trash." Regardless of the players' final thoughts about the game, most were very resistant to the switch to Abby in the middle of the game and felt that they had to force themselves to change their opinion of the new player character to enjoy playing the game again. However, not all players were willing or able to overcome the emotional hurdle, and the intense reactions to Abby's character generated a litany of negative reviews, even going so far as to cause some players to quit playing the game altogether.

These passionate responses to the game prove the power of *The Last of Us* to teach players to bridge the gap between digital entities and physical effects. By playing as Abby, the player ends up helping her get to Joel and later Ellie, thus effectively having players enact violence unto themselves. They become victimized by their own violent actions, and this makes them understandably angry and resistant to playing as Abby again. As Welsh writes:

The challenge for game makers is less often to convince players to overcome an aversion to on-screen violence as it is to get them to attribute worth, value, and significance to an arrangement of pixels.

Regardless of positive or negative opinions of Abby in *The Last of Us: Part II*, reactions to the story and character change were strong enough to elicit real actions in the physical world. Highlighting this connection between the digital and the physical is essential to recognize the extensive emotional violence that occurs online every day. On many social media platforms, people are reduced to profile pictures and one sentence bios. For many, they are represented only by their comments on a particular post or topic, and this anonymity makes it easier to ignore the nuances of personality and history that are inherent to any human being. We become like NPCs in a video game. The effects of Abby's reception highlighted the ability of "an arrangement of pixels" to influence the feelings of real people, and how our own digital actions, even when buffered through the acts of fictional characters, can have substantial effects on our own emotions and decision-making. It is both empowering and terrifying to realize that we have this power, just by having access to a screen.

 WITH VIRTUAL POWER COMES REAL RESPONSIBILITY

Ultimately, one of the goals of Naughty Dog's series was to examine the nature of violence and the ways in which violent agency hurts both user and victim. By having the player become the victims of their own computerized violence, the games highlight the bridge between digital violence and real pain, forcing the player to look through the anonymizing veil of the screen.

As we increasingly live our lives in online environments and interact with one another through screens of various sizes, it is of utmost importance that we are able to recognize in the digital display the weight and value of human life, even if all we ever know is the outline of a pixelated silhouette.

The importance of Welsh's argument cannot be understated, especially with the dramatic increase in online interactions propelled by the COVID-19 pandemic. As we saw from the real reactions to Abby, the digital sphere has a deep relationship with the physical, and online violence has very real effects on both perpetrator and victim. To be clear, this is not to say that one should never enjoy violent video games. In fact, *The Last of Us* and *The Last of Us: Part II* prove that violent games are uniquely poised to teach us about nonviolence by confronting the player the specifically bloody medium. By diluting violent action game mechanics with pacifist puzzle elements, the games can argue that nonviolent agency is essential to human existence, even within a setting where violence is necessary for survival.

Naughty Dog's hidden instruction calls for awareness — that we are conscious of the ignorance around violent agency. We can still have fun killing hundreds of nameless enemies and infected, as long as we remember our enjoyment of digital violence is due to the careful curation of the experience to remove the effects of reality. Players should always be aware of the filters that are inherent in the genre, and that violence outside of video games — digital or otherwise — is guaranteed to have terrible effects on all parties involved.

To end with a final look at *The Last of Us*, notice that the Molotov cocktail and the first aid kit in the game require the exact same crafting materials, a combination of alcohol and rags. While this may have been created solely for balancing purposes, it still offers the player an interesting perspective: given the same resources, one could either use them to enact violence or to heal. Given the powerful tools of digital technology, we can establish our personal agency with violence or nonviolence and, just like in the game, the final choice is up to us.

About the Author

ROY WANG, MA received his master's in English from Boston University in 2021, specializing in graphic novels. As expected, he loves analyzing nerd culture through academic lenses, and believes that the media we consume shapes us just as much as we shape it. In his free time, when he isn't reading comics or playing video games, you can find him either sewing or working on his 6-year long, homebrew Dungeons and Dragons campaign.

References

Druckmann, N., Newman, A., & Margenau, K. (Directors). (2020). *The Last of Us Part II*. [Video Game]. Naughty Dog.

Erb, V., Lee, S., & Yim Doh, Y. (2021). Player-Character Relationship and Game Satisfaction in Narrative Game: Focus on Player Experience of Character Switch in *The Last of Us Part II*. *Frontiers in Psychology, 12.* https://doi.org/10.3389/fpsyg.2021.709926

Harilal, S. (2018). Playing in the Continuum: Moral Relativism in The Last of Us. *[sic], 9*(1). https://doi.org/10.15291/sic/1.9.lc.7

Kim, S. Y. (2022). Getting Over the Fear of Murder: Video Game Violence and the Ethics of Empowerment in The Last of Us. In S. Choe (Ed.), *The Palgrave Handbook of Violence in Film and Media* (pp. 355-377). Springer International Publishing AG. https://doi.org/10.1007/978-3-031-05390-0_18

Pötzsch, H. (2017). Selective Realism: Filtering Experiences of War and Violence in First- and Third-Person Shooters. *Games & Culture, 12*(2), 156-178. https://doi.org/10.1177/1555412015587802

Straley, B., & Druckmann, N. (Directors). (2013). *The Last of Us*. [Video Game]. Naughty Dog.

Welsh, T. J. (2016). *Mixed Realism*. University of Minnesota Press. https://muse.jhu.edu/book/49341.

NAVIGATING POSTTRAUMATIC GROWTH IN *THE LAST OF US* FANDOM: THE POWER OF ONE-SIDED CONNECTIONS

ADAM BALDOWSKI

"I guess no matter how hard you try, you can't escape your past,"
—Joel, The Last of Us

Few things bring people together like popular culture. Films, television shows, books, comics, video games, and more, offer infinite ways for individuals to connect. The power of such media to resonate with individuals and evoke emotional responses has been an area of study for researchers for decades, and the connections formed by fans to both the media source and the larger fan communities have shown to have a profound and largescale impact, shaping experiences and emotional well-being.

The Last of Us is one such story — an iconic video game series, later adapted into a television show, that has captivated fans worldwide with its depiction of life after trauma. Beyond the screen, however, there is a world of positive psychological impact on fans and fan communities. This impact creates opportunities for camaraderie and collective engagement, which contribute to personal growth, resilience, and positive change among individuals who have experienced trauma or adversity.

At the heart of fandom is a duality of connections — both one-sided and communal. On one hand, there are profound emotional bonds forged between fans and fictional characters. These one-sided relationships, known as parasocial relationships, are more than just casual admiration; they are intimate and often therapeutic connections that offer solace, understanding, and even healing to fans facing their own real-world struggles. On the other hand, we find relationships within the fandom community, offering individual fans a chance to come together to share their passion, stories, and support for one another.

 FANDOM AS SOCIAL SUPPORT AND A CATALYST FOR POSTTRAUMATIC GROWTH

Fandoms offer a unique form of social support and community by providing a space for fans to share experiences, provide and receive support, and collectively explore themes such as resilience, growth, and moral dilemma — all themes found in the series *The Last of Us*.

But what does it mean to be a fan and to belong to a particular fandom? According to media psychology scholar Cynthia Vinney, PhD, a fan is an individual who is loyal to a specific interest, such as sports, celebrity, movies, video games, and more. Fans demonstrate enthusiasm about, and supportive of, something or someone. Being a part of a fandom means belonging to a community that shares a deep enthusiasm and love for a specific piece of media or franchise.

Media scholar Henry Jenkins outlined five levels of engagement fandoms take when interacting with a particular form of popular culture. These levels are:
1. Relationship to the mode of reception
2. Involvement of critical and interpretive practices
3. Encouragement of viewer activism
4. Production of content for the interest of the fan community

Function as a social community

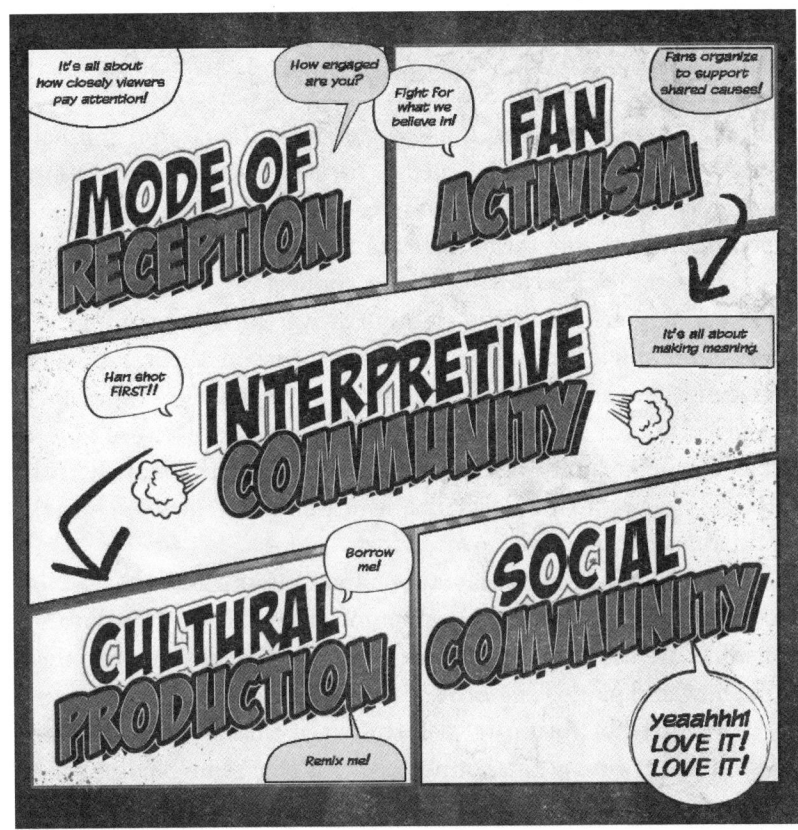

Figure 1

These five levels offer a look at how fans approach their collective interests and connect with one another. Jenkins wrote about fan culture:

> *I am not claiming that there is anything particularly empowering about the text's fans embrace. I am, however, claiming that there is something empowering about what fans do with those texts in the process of assimilating them to the particulars of their lives. Fandom celebrates not exceptional texts but rather exceptional readings (though its interpretive practices make it impossible to maintain a clear or precise distinction between the two).*

Jenkins argues that fans will maintain a certain intensity about a particular form of media, form certain interpretations, engage socially with others who share their interests, and make meaning from the material to relate back to their own lives.

For fans of The *Last of Us*, a connection with the characters was made through the rich narrative conveyed through the game play and overall story. Players focus on the relationship between Ellie and Joel, their individual and collective trauma, and the growth each made throughout the game. Fans were able to expanded upon their personal connections with the launch of the television series in January 2023, which breathed new life into the character's players had grown to love.

Jenkins goes on to say that fan communities are "self-organizing groups" that derive meaning from the very media they consume. We see this behavior in online fan forums for the television show and game, *The Last of Us*.

On a Reddit forum (r/thelastofus), a thread featured a discussion about how a fan connected with the game's portrayal of post-traumatic stress disorder (PTSD). Fans discussed the importance of such a connection. User Illex, who started the thread, wrote, "As someone who suffers from PTSD, I really connected with the game's portrayal of trauma." This fan found a connection to the game and how trauma was portrayed, resulting in a deeper connection to the overall narrative. By posting on Reddit, they were also able to connect with the larger *Last of Us* fanbase. On the same thread, user greekfiah responded to Illex:

> *Since you said you suffer from PTSD. Do you or did you ever had [sic] trouble with mirrors? (genuine question). When you go to Joel's house, if I remember correctly, there are no mirrors. (Maybe because of trauma) and when you go back to the farmhouse to find it empty, if you put Ellie in front of the mirror in the bathroom, she will keep turning her head and won't look at herself. While in any other part of the game she does.*

Greekgiah's theory about mirrors caused other users to engage in how deep the story felt and offer praise to the developers for taking their time with production.

The discussion on the Reddit thread resulted in users commenting on Illex's original post and supporting one another in their reactions to the game. Illex finishes their post by stating, "The game understands, sympathetically, but without judging or condoning, precisely how truly fucked up, confused, battered, and compulsively shameful victims of unresolved trauma are. And I love it for that." Others also commented on how they felt seen, and how important it was for trauma to be represented in a way that felt nonjudgemental.

Licensed Clinical Social Worker Joel Black writes about the portrayal of trauma in the television version of *The Last of Us*. He writes:

> *This show illustrates how the effects of traumatic events change the way the characters interact with their environment. The symptoms cause interference and avoidance that affect their ability to be effective in certain situations.*

It motivates their behaviors and is present in how they manage their relationships with others.

What Black describes here is the relationship people have to trauma and how trauma can negatively impact their lives. With work and resilience, personal growth can happen despite the trauma experienced.

In *The Last of Us* game, we see the character of Joel grow in subtle ways between the first and second game through the design and decorating of his living space. In the first game, his living space was bleak and dark, but in the second game, more personal items hang on the walls and the space has a warmer, more inviting feel. In TV series, Joel grows to embrace his protective side after losing those closest to him, taking on the father figure to Ellie and becoming her protector in the end.

The trauma Joel endures throughout the first game and at the start of the television series is enough to give anyone pause. Joel kept moving forward. Yes, he lived/lives with trauma, but he found strength in the trauma which allowed him to grow.

POSTTRAUMATIC GROWTH

Traumatic experiences can cause an individual to develop of a diagnosable mood disorder known as posttraumatic stress disorder (PTSD). PTSD can present in many ways, but broadly speaking occurs when a person has difficulty recovering from the direct experience or witnessing of a traumatic event. It should be noted that not all trauma leads to PTSD, and everyone responds to trauma differently. Just as trauma can lead to negative impacts, growth is also possible.

In 1995 researchers Tedeschi and Calhoun introduced the term posttraumatic growth as an alternative outcome to the documented negative effects of traumatic experiences. Posttraumatic growth (PTG) is a psychological concept that emerged from studying the positive psychological change in individuals who have faced trauma and adversity. Research has found PTG is not merely the resilience to bounce back from difficult experiences; it is the profound process of personal growth and positive change that can arise from trauma and adversity. PTG can arise in many forms and be vast in scope, and is unique to the individual experiencing it. For some it may be exploring a hidden talent, finding faith, deepening personal relationships, among many pursuits.

In their research, Tedeschi and Calhoun identified five areas where growth can occur. These areas are:
1. Changes in how they relate to other people
2. Recognition of new opportunities, priorities, or pathways in life
3. Greater appreciation for the value of one's own life, and life in general
4. Recognition of one's own strength
5. Spiritual or existential development

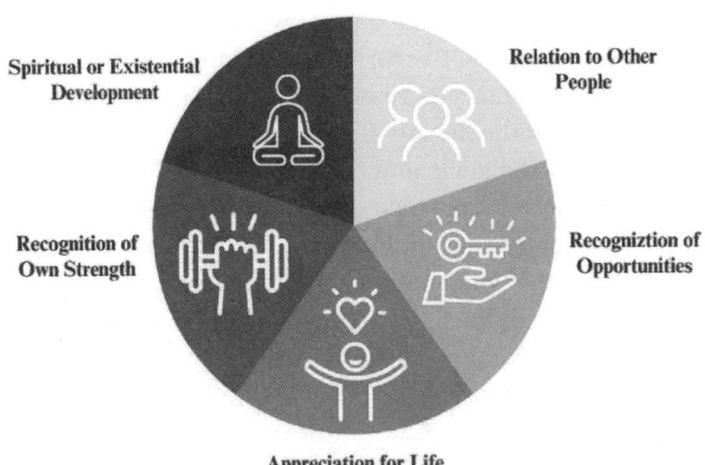

Figure 2

In the context of *The Last of Us* fandom, PTG manifests in unique ways, showing the ability of fictional narratives and shared experiences to inspire hope, resilience, and personal development. Joel finds new meaning in life, new priorities, and a new role taking care of Ellie — something he thought he would never do after the loss of his daughter. He pushes through his negative beliefs about people to learn to trust again, building a support system, allowing him to grow and move forward.

Journalist Victoria Stokes interviewed clinical psychologist Dr. Marianne Trent and environmental psychologist Lee Chambers, noting that while PTG can generate gratitude for life and place new focus on relationships, the ability to grow from trauma can depend on several life factors. These factors include a support system, personality traits, the ability to integrate trauma, and the development of a new belief system.

In *The Last of Us,* Joel showed growth through personal change and strength in how he has chosen to live. When we first meet Joel after his trauma, his life feels bleak and hopeless, but through his journey we, the audience, see glimmers of light in his life, like his apartment having a more welcoming feel. This is not to say that Joel would not experience anything negative from his trauma, but instead has progressed to learned how to make something positive from the negative.

Fans of both the game and the series have found connection through both the relationships depicted in the game/series, but also the relationships they build in real life.

Ian O'Rourke of Fandomlife notes, "…it (the television series) presents this beautiful hell, in that no matter how much it makes you cry or uncomfortable it doesn't transgress over the line of you not wanting to watch it."

The connections formed are parasocial in nature, meaning they are one-sided— where the player and audience, form a bond with the character, but the character is not aware the fan exists.

 PARASOCIAL RELATIONSHIPS AND
POSTTRAUMATIC GROWTH IN
THE LAST OF US

It is difficult to talk about fandom without first talking about the connection a fan has to a particular story, character, or series. These relationships tend to be one-sided, because one half of the interaction is either fictional or significantly removed from their own day-to-day life (e.g. a celebrity). According to social psychologist Karen Dill-Shackelford, parasocial relationships are one-sided connections that individuals form with media personalities or fictional characters, often from a form of pop culture such as books, television, film, or video games. Dill-Shackelford and other social psychologists have expanded the definition of parasocial relationships to include connections and interactions, which illustrates the difference between real-world social relationships and parasocial relationships.

In video games like The *Last of Us,* fans can interact with characters by controlling them on screen and making decisions to move the story forward. When games are translated into other mediums, fans of the story can see the characters they play come to life in a new format. In January 2023, fans of the game *The Last of Us* were able to watch a story they have grown to love come to life on the small screen.

In the context of *The Last of Us,* characters who undergo severe trauma might demonstrate PTG through their personal transformations, evolving relationships, and altered life perspectives. Players of the game can witness and be a part of a character's PTG through the development of the character, moral decision making, survival skills, and empathy. The narrative depicts how characters navigate their trauma, leading to potential growth and change in line with PTG principles. In the world of *The Last of Us*, parasocial relationships between players and characters like Ellie and Joel can serve as powerful catalysts for posttraumatic growth. Fans can, in turn, communicate and gather both digitally and in person to discuss their thoughts and feelings about the content — colloquially known as the "water cooler effect."

THE WATER COOLER EFFECT AND FAN COMMUNITIES

The term "water cooler effect" (WCE) refers to the informal social interactions and discussions that often occurring in casual settings (like around a water cooler in an office). In fandoms, the WCE describes the phenomenon where fans gather online or in person to discuss their favorite media content, share experiences, and build connections.

Since much of the research on WCE revolves around corporate and organizational structures, there is little research linking the model with fan spaces. There is evidence that the traditional water cooler space has moved online with the advent of social media and other online forums.

In fan spaces, such as online forums, social media groups, or fan conventions, the water cooler effect might manifest as discussions about shared interests, exchange of ideas, or casual conversations about related topics. These interactions can foster community building and a sense of belonging among fans.

According to Lynn Zubernis, PhD, fans find a positive experience in gathering both virtually and in person, noting that "neurotransmitters such as dopamine and endorphins foster a feeling of communal belonging, with bigger groups creating bigger effects." Being a fan creates identity within a group and allows for an individual to feel supported, which can reduce feelings of loneliness and other negative traits.

For fans of *The Last of Us*, a connection to both the characters and the community took root after episode three of the series aired. This episode depicts a romantic story between characters Bill and Frank. Bill and Frank represented something not often depicted in mainstream media — a healthy, loving same-sex relationship. This representation was not lost to fans and sparked much discussion online. In an interview with Pink News' Marcus Wratten, Matt Harwick — the co-founder of queer gaming group London Gaymers — became emotional upon seeing gay representation outside of how the gay community is traditionally represented. Harwick mentioned representation in the game is subtle, but noticeable by those in the LGBTQ+ community. In the TV series, Harwick notes Bill and Frank's story was about two people in love, and did not focus on their sexuality or controversial subjects often depicted in LGBTQ+ storylines.

Fans of the series went online to sites such as Reddit and Twitter to express their emotions in what they witnessed. Expressions of heartache, sadness, surprise, and despair were expressed, but all in recognition of the inclusive nature of the storyline. This experience compliments O'Rourke's sentiment that the series paints a picture of a "beautiful hell," where characters find strength and happiness in the bleakest of circumstances. Through adversity and trauma, growth occurred both for the characters and the audience.

 COPING STRATEGIES AND SHARED EXPERIENCES

Within fan communities, individuals often find coping strategies and support from those who have undergone similar experiences. Whether directly, or indirectly, fans can share their own coping mechanisms and stories of growth — contributing to a sense of shared experience and solidarity. These shared experiences can inspire others and contribute to the PTG of individuals within the community.

Fans who have played the game can bond over their shared emotional experiences, discussing how the game's storytelling impacted them personally. Sharing these experiences can help individuals process their own emotions and feel understood by others who have gone through similar journeys.

However, fan interactions go far beyond online platforms such as message boards. Fans express themselves creatively by generating art and stories, unique to their fan interest. For fans of *The Last of Us*, these creative endeavors allow fans to reinterpret and reimagine the world created by the game and televisions series; characters and events provide a therapeutic way to process their feelings and share their interpretations with others. This creative outlet keeps in line with the fourth layer of Henry Jenkins' five layers of fandom — Production of content for the interest of the fan community.

Beyond creating art or writing stories, sometimes fans take their love for their fan interest to in-person experiences by participating in cosplay and attending conventions. These gatherings provide opportunities for fans to connect with others in real life, exchange stories, and display their dedication to the game and series. Conventions also often host panel discussions and Q&A sessions with the source material's creators, extending a sense of community and shared experiences.

Juliette Burton at the MQ Foundation writes that costume play(cosplay) allows for fans to experience validation, connection, and affirmation. Cosplay can go beyond looking like an exact copy of a particular character and allow the fan to put their own spin on the costume to feel greater self-representation. For example, a fan may choose to gender swap a character to feel more comfortable in how they are represented.

According to Cityscape Counseling, cosplay can be used to build self-esteem and confidence, allowing fans to dress up as someone else and participate in a community they find meaningful. Outcomes like developing a talent for outward expression, learning to make costumes, or simply finding comfort in acting as someone else are all potential ways PTG can manifest. Of course, it is not as simple as dressing up as a character, but instead revolves around community, identity building, and feelings of safety. Cosplay can help with anxiety by providing a mask to make social interactions easier to manage.

Through the larger fan community, fans can move beyond the one-sided relationships they form with the characters and lean on one another for support. By analyzing fans' engagement with the narrative, character development, and thematic exploration across both the game and TV interpretation of *The Last of Us*, we can shed light on the transformative potential of fandom in relation to PTG. Fan connections foster empathy, understanding, and personal growth in the aftermath of trauma and adversity, but much of the growth also relies on the willingness and resilience of the individual themselves.

Through the lens of PTG, we unveiled the psychological impact of both the one-sided relationships and the communal bonds that define the vibrant fandom of *The Last of Us*. Moving through trauma is never easy, but as Joel said in the closing moments of the game, "I struggled for a long time with survivin.' No matter what, you keep finding something to fight for."

About the Author

ADAM BALDOWSKI, PH.D., MA, LMHC, CGT is a Certified Geek Therapist in Orlando, Florida, whose therapeutic work includes sexual trauma, dissociative disorders, life transition, and LGBTQIA+ experiences. Adam identifies as part of the LGBTQIA+ community and is a long-time nerd and geek who studies the connection between media, the human condition, and how people make meaning from the media they engage. Adam believes the best way to reach clients theoretically is to speak the language of the client's interests. While talk therapy is the main format used in their therapeutic sessions, Adam also incorporates elements of geek culture into their work, including gaming, comic books, film, music, anime, and more.

References

Black, J. (2023, March 10). *Understanding trauma in the last of US*. Redemption Counseling, LLC - Mental health, counseling, therapy, addiction, depression, anxiety in MO and IL. https://redemptiontherapist.com/understanding-trauma-in-the-last-of-us/

Burton, J. (2023, November 1). *Costume, cosplay and dressing up: Fashion and Mental Health*. MQ Mental Health Research. https://www.mqmentalhealth.org/costume-cosplay-and-dressing-up-fashion-and-mental-health/?lang=en_us#:~:text=Experiences%20of%20validation%2C%20community%20connections,within%20it%20find%20a%20family.

Cynthia Vinney, P. (2022, June 9). *What is the effect of long-term fandom?*. Verywell Mind. https://www.verywellmind.com/what-is-the-effect-of-long-term-fandom-5296129

O'Rorke, I. (2023, March 18). *The last of Us*. Fandomlife. https://www.fandomlife.net/5527/

Illex. (2020, June 27). R/thelastofus - as someone who suffers from PTSD, I really connected ... https://www.reddit.com/r/thelastofus/comments/hgrsyn/as_someone_who_suffers_from_ptsd_i_really/

Jenkins, H. (2006). Chapter 6: Interactive Audiences? The "collective Intelligence" of Media Fans. In *Fans, Bloggers, and Gamers: Exploring Participatory Culture*. essay, New York University.

Jenkins, H. (2013). *Textual poachers: Television fans and participatory culture*. Routledge.

Shackleford, K. E., Walker, K., & Dean, K. (2021). *Real characters: The psychology of parasocial relationships with media characters*. Fielding University Press.

Tedeschi, R. G., & Calhoun, L. G. (2013, September 24). *Tempered by fire*. Psychology Today. https://www.psychologytoday.com/us/blog/beyond-resilience/201309/tempered-fire

Tilton, S. (2019, March 3). *Jenkins' five levels of fandom activity*. Cyber Means Pilot. https://shanetilton.com/jenkins-five-levels-of-fandom-activity/

Wratten, M. (2023, February 12). *Gamers reflect on the last of us giving Bill and Frank the Love Story They deserve*. PinkNews. https://www.thepinknews.com/2023/02/12/the-last-of-us-bill-frank-gamers-reaction/

THE NARRATIVE OF TRAUMA: HOW *THE LAST OF US* PORTRAYS PTSD AND TRAUMA

MICHELLE "MICHIE" LECCESE

"There are a million ways we should've died before today, and a million ways we can die before tomorrow. But we fight, for every second we get to spend with each other. Whether it's two minutes or two days, we don't give that up."
—Riley, *The Last of Us: Left Behind*

"The paradox of trauma is that it has both the power to destroy and the power to transform and resurrect."
—Peter A. Levine, PhD.

THE WEIGHT OF SURVIVAL: JOEL'S EMOTIONAL TURMOIL

"I struggled for a long time with surviving. And, no matter what, you keep finding something to fight for."
—Joel Miller, *The Last of Us: Part I*

The opening sequence of *The Last of Us: Part I* is arguably one of gaming's most impactful and heart-wrenching scenes. A cinematic masterpiece that follows characters from normal everyday life to one upheaved by chaos and zombie-like infected humans, *The Last of Us* captures the essence of a traumatic event, as well as the aftermath of that trauma on the main protagonists. When we first meet Joel Miller, he is a charismatic, fun-loving, goofy father to his daughter, Sarah. The two share a humorous and laid-back moment in celebration of Joel's birthday and all is seemingly well in the world.

Unfortunately, this version of Joel and this moment of peace are both short lived. Players are now thrown into the world of the outbreak and witness Sarah's death, thus changing the trajectory of the main protagonist, and the world he lives in, for the remainder of the narrative.

The initial outbreak of the cordyceps fungus constitutes a massive, world-wide traumatic event, as defined by the Diagnostic and Statistical Manual, 5th Edition (DSM-5), in that individuals in *The Last of Us* face "actual or threatened death, serious injury, or sexual violence." Trauma, broadly defined, is a psychological and emotional response to an event or series of events that are distressing or harmful to an individual or society. Events typically categorized as traumatic can include anything from natural disasters to the loss of a loved one, and are more severe than stress individuals experience on a daily basis. In this context, the rapid spread of the cordyceps infection acts as a singular global trauma.

Like the real-life events that occurred in early 2020 when the COVID-19 virus spread throughout the planet, the world of the cordyceps outbreak immediately shuts down any sense of normalcy, and modern life as Joel knows it ceases to exist. In *The Last of Us*, governmental services are not equipped to deal with the outbreak or the massive emigration of civilian suburbs. Cell service is disconnected, leaving everyone unable to connect with loved ones to ensure their safety. Water, food, and basic living necessities all become scarce, creating widespread panic and conflict amongst communities. Individuals constantly fear being infected themselves and even more so doubt the honesty and integrity of those around them. The world is engulfed in chaos, leaving behind more than just destruction of property. The characters in *The Last of Us* exchange physical baggage for psychological baggage, which they carry with them always.

Trauma affects all aspects of an individual's life and can be categorized into various types, including: acute trauma (single event), chronic trauma (prolonged or repeated exposure), and complex trauma (exposure to varied and multiple traumatic events). In the case of *The Last of Us*, the main character has faced multiple acute traumas (such as the loss of Sarah for Joel, and the loss of Riley for Ellie), as well as chronic trauma caused by the continuous stress of the infection destroying humanity. While it is common to experience mild levels of trauma and stress, continuous and repeated exposure to trauma without intervention or treatment can lead to psychological disorders such as posttraumatic stress disorder (PTSD), acute stress disorder, anxiety, and/or depression.

PTSD is the result of a traumatic event that leaves an individual with such an emotional impact that they feel the effects of the trauma months — or even years — after the original event(s). While symptoms of PTSD vary from individual to individual, psychologists and clinicians place symptoms into four main categories: intrusive symptoms, avoidance symptoms, arousal and reactivity symptoms, and negative changes in cognition and mood.

Category	Symptoms
Intrusive	Flashbacks, nightmares, unwelcomed distressing thoughts
Avoidance	Avoiding people, places, things that remind individuals of the traumatic event(s), emotional numbing

Arousal and Reactivity	Hyperarousal, easily startled, difficulty sleeping or maintaining sleep, always "on-edge," restlessness
Negative Changes in Cognition and Mood	Negative thoughts, memory issues, blunted emotions, difficulty expressing positive emotions

* Adapted from the DSM-5 entry on Posttraumatic Stress Disorder

Over 20 years pass since the initial outbreak and Sarah's death in the game. Players now witness an aging Joel startled awake by a knock on the door. The disgruntled and rugged man has clearly changed as he speaks to the woman, Tess, who he lets into his apartment. Joel is no longer the fun-loving, goofy father figure we had seen with Sarah. Rather, he is cold, harsh, and direct as he discusses the upcoming job with Tess. Joel is now a man hardened by the loss of his daughter and the destruction of his life as he knew it. Faced with the continuous traumas of the outside world, still littered with the infected, players witness several key changes in Joel's mood and affect. These changes in mood include emotional numbness, cynicism and distrust, isolation and withdrawal, loss of hope, aggression, and risk aversion, all of which are symptoms widely displayed by individuals suffering from PTSD.

Many of these specific changes in affect and mood can be seen when Joel first meets Ellie, and in how he continues to interact with her throughout the game. When Joel initially meets Ellie, she is nothing but a commodity to him — cargo to transport and money in his wallet. It does not matter to him that Ellie is a preteen, similar in age to his daughter, nor that she is alone in the world. She just needs to be transported safely so that Joel can get on with his life. This difficulty connecting and emotional numbness acts as a protective barrier to future loss. By never letting anyone get close to him, Joel can ensure that he will not be hurt by another death. Joel's inability to form new connections means that his support network is small. He is hesitant to trust others — often assuming they have malicious intent or ulterior motives — and rarely shows any emotion other than anger. This is evident by the fact that he has very few close confidants besides Tess. Even with Tess, Joel is gruff, emotionless, and displays a stoic demeanor, while refraining from openly expressing grief or vulnerability. This emotional shield is an avoidance mechanism that is common among individuals suffering from untreated PTSD.

SURVIVING SOLITUDE: JOEL'S TALE OF ISOLATION AND MISTRUST

Joel's relationship with his brother, Tommy, is also strained, and characterized by a level of cynicism that adds additional burden to an already traumatized man. In a world where no one can be trusted, it feels equally cruel to be at odds with direct family and friends. This distrust, paired with Joel's anger, showcases negative changes in thinking and mood from 20 years prior, when he lost his daughter. Losing Sarah stays with him throughout the game, no matter how much Joel would like to pretend it does not; suppressing these feelings has a deep impact on his future ability to heal and move past his trauma.

Isolation, distrust, strained relationships, and cynicism create additional exaggerated and irrational thought patterns known as cognitive distortions, which make treating or overcoming trauma additionally challenging. These cognitive distortions (e.g. personalization such as "Sarah's death was my fault") blur the line between reality of the moment and the shadows cast by the lack of safety in the past. With Ellie, Joel's cognitive distortions lead him to believe it is easier to look at her as an object of trade and to keep a pessimistic outlook on a vaccine being created by her immunity than to have any glimmer of hope that something might change.

Individuals with unhealed trauma tend to struggle with thinking past the next few steps to a more hopeful future. Oftentimes, survivors of traumatic events reject the notion of hope in favor of avoiding re-traumatization or negative emotions caused by potential vulnerabilities. Throughout most of *The Last of Us*, Joel is unable to imagine a future beyond immediate survival. Even when Joel learns that Ellie is immune to the virus, his outlook on the future of humanity, and of Ellie herself, is narrowed and bleak. While it may seem harsh for Joel to react this way to Ellie, his limited outlook acts as a necessary coping mechanism for his trauma. By narrowing his perspective to only the immediate challenge of surviving, Joel ensures the safety of himself (and assumedly Tess) both physically and psychologically in this post-apocalyptic world.

 GAME OVERLOAD: *THE LAST OF US* AND FIGHT OR FLIGHT

During traumatic events, an individual's body goes into what is commonly known as the "flight or fight" response. This physiological reaction is a survival mechanism that prepares individuals to either confront a danger (fight), or flee from it (flight), by activating the body's sympathetic nervous system. When the sympathetic nervous system activates, floods of various hormones, including epinephrine (adrenaline) and cortisol, are released into the body. The release of adrenaline has many physiological effects — increasing heart rate, elevating blood pressure, dilating pupils, increasing respiratory rate, and dulling pain receptors. The release of cortisol acts in tandem with adrenaline to sustain the body's heightened state of arousal over time. Blood is redirected to major muscle groups to enhance speed and strength, while non-essential bodily functions (like digesting) are suppressed to allow maximal physical advantage and increase chances of survival. The increased flow of blood and oxygen to the brain provides the individual with elevated cognitive functions, ensuring they are alert in their decision-making.

The Last of Us constantly shows the main protagonists in this state of heightened arousal at various moments of intense action, providing players with an insight into these physiological changes. The game also shows players the consequences of chronic stress and dysregulation that come with repeated exposure to fight or flight responses. More specifically, the game illustrates what happens to an individual when this response is never turned off. Expecting and preparing for the worst at any given moment is the result of feeling unsafe and helpless during the initial traumatic event. This insecurity and loss of control constitutes a key factor in development of hypervigilance and anxiety. Hypervigilance and increased state of arousal are both survival and coping mechanisms that lead traumatized individuals to constantly be ready to act in the time of any future crisis. While an effective method of quickly preparing Joel and Ellie for fights with clickers, bloaters, or enemy humans, this perpetual state of readiness caused by overuse of the fight or flight response leads to exhaustion, anxiety, and overall restlessness.

Chronic activation of this response can also contribute to various stress-related disorders if not treated properly, and affect an individual's normal everyday functions, such as maintaining proper sleep. Players see this in the cutscenes of Joel's restless insomnia, his excessive attempts to stay awake with medication, and his jumpy reactions to potential threats.

WATCH OUT: JOEL'S AVOIDANCE AND REACTIVITY TO SARAH

"Do you even realize what your life means?"
—Joel (*The Last of Us: Part I*)

Yet another aspect of PTSD that is highlighted throughout the game is the persistent and active avoidance Joel engages with regarding his own trauma. Throughout the entirety of *The Last of Us*, Joel does not discuss Sarah with anyone, and actively refuses to talk about the time before the outbreak; this gives players a firsthand account of the intensity of his traumatic memories and triggers.

A particularly noteworthy example is how Joel reacts to others that bring up his daughter. When Joel is reunited with his brother, Tommy, Tommy presents Joel with a photo of Joel and Sarah together at a soccer tournament.

What should have been a happy, even if mildly somber, moment quickly becomes a an avoidance tactic. He bluntly states that he does not want the picture, and he avoids directly looking at the picture as he quickly returns the photo back to Tommy. We see Joel's attempt to distance himself emotionally from the traumatic memories linked to his daughter's death. By rejecting the picture of the two of them, Joel purposely avoids an emotional trigger and does not face the intense emotions associated with his daughter's death.

For those struggling through a traumatic event, even small, inconspicuous objects can be triggers for pain, grief, and sorrow. A memento of a lost loved one could be a loving heartfelt memory, or it could spiral an individual into intense guilt, depression, anxiety, and sometimes rage. Flashbacks are common amongst emotional and physical triggers, and we see these reactions from Joel whenever Sarah or his past are mentioned. Immediately after Joel rejects the picture, he asks Tommy to take Ellie the rest of the journey. He again attempts to avoid loss — this time the loss of Ellie — even if this is not what he says out loud. Rather, instead of expressing his anxieties and fears to his brother, he berates Tommy and attempts to guilt him into taking Ellie the rest of the way. Only when Ellie is in danger from a fight between bandits and Tommy's men does Tommy witness the love and affection that Joel has developed for Ellie. This tenderness towards Ellie and worry for her safety leads Tommy to think that his brother asking him to take Ellie off his hands was not in an effort to simply get rid of her, but an attempt to safeguard his emotions and avoid losing yet another daughter figure. Due to this clear affection, Tommy agrees to take Ellie and spare his brother any more pain. The pair would leave in the morning without Joel, and Joel would have once again successfully indulged the avoidance tendencies fed by his trauma.

Once Ellie learns that Tommy is now taking her to the Firefly lab location rather than Joel, she takes off in a rage. When Joel and Tommy eventually find her in a nearby outlook, players find Ellie sitting in the room of a teenage girl who used to live there. She laments at the seemingly pointless struggles teenage girls had before the outbreak, such as boys and what skirt went with what shirt. Players recognize that Sarah feels grief at what her own life could have been. Joel immediately ignores Ellie's comments, and argues with her instead about the worth of her life. After this long, arduous journey, the two of them have started to trust and even care for one another. In their argument, Ellie immediately calls out Joel directly on his trauma, asking him if he is afraid of losing her like he lost others. Joel deflects her question by recounting the close calls the two of them have had and reiterating that Tommy knows the area better and will be a much better asset to her for the rest of the trip. Joel turns away, his jaw clenched as he grapples with his anger towards the situation. His emotional responses are blunted by his inability to express any emotion besides anger. His pain is masked by the anger that he is attached to Ellie — and the fear that he has of losing her.

As he turns away, Ellie's voice drops into a sincerer and sorrowful tone to tell him that "I am not her, you know," before divulging to him that Maria told her about his daughter. Quickly, Joel warns Ellie that she is walking on "some mighty thin ice" with that topic. Rather than leaving it alone, Ellie addresses the fact that they both have had significant losses in their lives. This triggers Joel further into claiming Ellie she does not understand loss. Ellie shouts back that she has grown to trust him and would be scared of going the rest of the trip with someone else. In a final attempt to shield himself from his own emotions, Joel bluntly tells Ellie that she is not his daughter, and he is not her dad. This is his final attempt to rid himself of Ellie by hurting her enough that she hates him.

Joel shutting down Ellie is a prime example of avoidant behavior. This is not a new phenomenon, but it is now a central aspect of the pair's relationship with trauma and each other. Joel has a visceral emotional response to Ellie comparing herself to Sarah. His active refusal to discuss his past, especially as it relates to his daughter, is a clear indication of his attempt to distance himself from that excruciating memory. Joel's defensive posture and his anger towards Ellie serve as emotional armor, guarding him from feeling his pain or acknowledging his bond with Ellie. As Ellie pierces through his emotional armor with her comparison of herself and Sarah, Joel resorts to a last-ditch effort to distance himself by using her abandonment and trust issues to hurt her.

Joel's attempt at hurting Ellie to is not malicious, nor was it a healthy response to a stressful situation. It was his way to avoid acknowledging the deep connection and bond that he has formed with Ellie through this journey. If Joel acknowledges their bond, he risks leaving himself open to potentially hurt— or more specifically, the pain of losing her. These actions are hallmark examples of avoidance behaviors common in individuals with PTSD. Ultimately, Joel decides to overcome his fear of losing Ellie and take her the rest of the way to the Fireflies, but in true Joel style, no additional sentiment or discussion is given as the two ride off with one another and leave Tommy behind. The incident is never mentioned again within the narrative, once again showcasing Joel's avoidance tendencies in response to any type of emotional stressor.

Despite Joel's emotional avoidance in his communication with Ellie, and his refusal of the photo from Tommy, the player can clearly see that he still wears the watch Sarah gave him for his birthday. Disregarding some forms of emotion while keeping a different object of sentimental value highlights the messy, inexplicable nature of trauma. The watch, broken at the exact time Sarah was shot to death, acts as a constant reminder that Joel failed in his parental role. Joel keeps the broken watch on his arm, but shies away from keeping memories such as pictures of his daughter with him. Many have theorized that the watch serves as a reminder of his failures and to keep surviving in the darkness, while the picture is a reminder of times before. Within this theory, it seems reasonable to accept that Joel is avoiding any remnants of his past joy to keep a level head with his trauma; a trauma that keeps him, in his mind, safe and moving forward.

Joel's refusal to keep Sarah's picture while keeping the broken watch also suggests a complex interplay of what is known as survivors' guilt. This intense type of emotional response occurs when individuals survive a traumatic event while others do not; in this case. Joel survived but his daughter was killed. The watch becomes a tangible representation of his survivor's guilt and a reminder that he persists and she does not. This can also be seen as a masochistic act, where Joel punishes himself for the death of his daughter, or to hold onto feelings of unworthiness. Trauma survivors may feel they do not deserve the life they now lead, especially if they perceive that other equally or more worthy individuals did not survive the same event. As a parent, Joel feels that he has failed in his duty to take care of his child, ultimately leading to feelings of low self-worth and difficulty finding joy in a world without Sarah. While it is unclear why Joel keeps the watch but not the photo of Sarah, it is evident that the trauma of the event and his feelings towards both Ellie and Sarah make Joel's character and story development more complicated and human.

INESCAPABLE ECHOES: ELLIE'S STRUGGLE WITH INTRUSIVE PTSD FLASHBACKS

"I guess no matter how hard you try, you can't escape your past."
—Joel Miller (*The Last of Us: Part I*)

The world of the infected is a hostile, temperamental, and, in more ways than not, a tragic life for those who endure its hardship. There is no doubt that the characters in *The Last of Us* have experienced tremendous amounts of trauma throughout the game's narrative. From the infection running rampant throughout the globe, to infighting when materials become scarce, there are many events that cause significant stress for Joel and Ellie. Ellie has multiple flashbacks in *The Last of Us: Part II* that leave her incapacitated. She replays Joel's brutal death and hears his screams of pain ring in her head. While these flashbacks happen several times throughout *The Last of Us: Part II*, one specific example demonstrates the strength of these intrusions: the barn scene.

Ellie and her partner Dina now live on a quiet farmstead with their child, JJ. The peaceful atmosphere is starkly different from the rest of the world players have encountered, and we see the characters experience tranquility. This peace is short lived, when the noise of a shovel clambering to the ground triggers an intense emotional and physical flashback for Ellie. A vision of Joel's head being smashed to the ground quickly follows the noisy shovel, and Ellie is left hyperventilating and stuck in a state of shock. Ellie is then mentally transported back to the location where Joel was murdered. Ellie finds herself standing at the top of a dark staircase overlooking a closed door, and upon recognizing the abandoned house, begins shaking her head while repeating "no no no." Joel's screams and pleas can be heard somewhere behind the closed door. Frantically, Ellie runs down the stairs, screaming for Joel, as her attempts to batter down the door with the entire force of her body fail, and the flashback ends. Ellie is back in the barn, huddled on the floor, screaming, hyperventilating, and completely unaware of the screaming infant in her arms. It is unclear how long Ellie has been incapacitated on the floor before her partner Dina comes to her aid helps ground Ellie back into reality. After a few moments, Ellie quickly apologizes for her actions, and Dina sits with her and their child while Ellie returns from her activated fight or flight state.

The barn sequence highlights the unpredictable nature of intrusive memories, demonstrating how even seemingly innocuous events can become intense triggers that plunge trauma victims back into the site of the original traumatic event. In this scene, Ellie experiences key elements of a PTSD flashback — hyperventilation, panic, and a dissociative state. She is unable to distinguish the present environment from the intrusive memory of her trauma. While she is physically in the barn, her psyche is trapped on the staircase of Joel's murder. In this flashback, Ellie is even in the clothes she wore the day of that trauma, emphasizing the transportation back to a previous time. Her physical response to move and help Joel indicate a need and want to change her past. In this instance, this flashback retraumatized Ellie and leaves her body in a state of hyperarousal and fear.

LOST IN TIME: ELLIE'S BARNYARD
FLASHBACK FIASCO

The uncertain duration of Ellie's flashback also highlights the dissociative nature of PTSD flashbacks. When Ellie comes to, she is no longer standing in the barn, but rather sitting on the floor against a hay bale screaming, crying, and unaware of the infant in her arms doing the same. It is not uncommon for individuals suffering from PTSD to lose track of time, to feel a distorted reality when experiencing a flashback, or to experience levels of depersonalization while in a dissociated state. Dissociation is a type of defense mechanism that creates a temporary disconnection from the overwhelming emotions and physical state of arousal caused by traumatic stimuli. Ellie's dissociation is clear in the barn scene, where she becomes completely unaware of the distressed child in her arms. Her inability to recognize the screaming child suggests a momentary disconnection from her own body and present environment, and illustrates the intense impact of her traumatic memory.

This scene shows how critical it is to have external support to ground individuals back into the present from these flashbacks and dissociative episodes. We see this in Dina's communication with Ellie as she is huddled and dissociated on the floor. Dina's use of precise language in telling Ellie where she is currently (e.g., "you're home") and direct instructions to look at Dina's face and breathe all help Ellie regain her footing in the present reality. Dina also takes a crucial step in removing the child from Ellie's arms to help regulate both the child's and Ellie's nervous systems. By removing the child, reminding Ellie of where she actually is, and giving clear instructions to Ellie, Dina supports Ellie in regulating herself. We see how Ellie's shoulders loosen, her breathing begins to slow, and her hand rests on her heart to give pressure to her chest. These exact steps are utilized in real-life situations and are proven to help individuals experiencing flashbacks get grounded back to reality. Dina's presence highlights the importance of social support in combating the feelings of isolation that are typical of those with PTSD.

"Endure and Survive" – Savage Starlight

What makes *The Last of Us* so compelling to players is how relatable and human the characters are. There are no "good guys" or "bad guys" to be seen — but rather a myriad of human faults, emotions, and traumatic events that lead humans to make mistakes, act on fear, and make rash or undeveloped decisions. Players bond with Joel and Ellie because they have faults and process their traumas in imperfect ways. Even when players do not agree with their decisions, the audience responds emotionally and understands the motives behind the actions. *The Last of Us* allows players to witness and directly experience the effects of trauma on the body and mind.

The ability to empathize with these characters makes *The Last of Us* franchise a memorable and emotional experience. It explores themes of loss, grief, famine, scarcity, and fear, and explores both physical and psychological trauma throughout the game. The various coping mechanisms that each individual character displays are authentic and realistic. The representation of trauma in this game is difficult to endure and heartbreaking to witness, but powerful in its that it is authenticity and accuracy. By catastrophizing the circumstances around each character's traumatic events, the game evokes intense emotions in players, and in doing so transforms passive consumers into informed advocates for trauma victims. Even in the darkest, most extreme circumstances — like t a worldwide outbreak — these characters find social support and eventually develop ways to handle their trauma, as imperfect as they may be. The experience of playing the game and traversing with these narratives is just as messy, meaningful, and transformative as the trauma it so poignantly portrays.

About the Author

MICHELLE "MICHIE" LECCESE, MA (she/her) is a PhD student in the Communications department at the University of Southern California. Michie received her Masters in Psychology from Pepperdine University and her Bachelors in Psychology and Disability Studies from UCLA. Her research focuses on the intersection of interactive media, prosocial behavior, and therapeutic practices: specifically focusing on video game play and resilience training for trauma survivors. She has held positions at Activision Blizzard on the User Research team, and as a fellow with the Center for Scholars and Storytellers at UCLA. Currently, Michie serves as an Adjunct Professor of Psychology at Pepperdine University.

Resources

American Psychiatric Association, D. S. M. T. F., & American Psychiatric Association. (2013). *Diagnostic and statistical manual of mental disorders: DSM-5* (Vol. 5, No. 5). Washington, DC: American psychiatric association.

Becker-Blease, K. A., & Freyd, J. J. (2005). Beyond PTSD: An evolving relationship between trauma theory and family violence research. *Journal of Interpersonal Violence, 20*(4), 403-411.

Boldi, A., & Rapp, A. (2022). Commercial video games as a resource for mental health: A systematic literature review. *Behaviour & Information Technology, 41*(12), 2654-2690.

Bryant, R. A., O'Donnell, M. L., Creamer, M., McFarlane, A. C., & Silove, D. (2011). Posttraumatic intrusive symptoms across psychiatric disorders. *Journal of Psychiatric Research, 45*(6), 842-847.

Creamer, M., Burgess, P., & Pattison, P. (1992). Reaction to trauma: a cognitive processing model. *Journal of abnormal psychology, 101*(3), 452.

Garland, C. (2018). *Understanding trauma: A psychoanalytical approach*. Routledge.

Herman, J. L. (1992). Complex PTSD: A syndrome in survivors of prolonged and repeated trauma. *Journal of traumatic stress, 5*(3), 377-391.

Hamblen, J., & Barnett, E. (2016). PTSD in children and adolescents. *National Center for PTSD, in www. ncptsd. org*.

Johnson, S. M. (2023). "Go. Just take him.": PTSD and the Player-Character Relationship in The Last of Us Part II. *Games and Culture, 18*(7), 855-867.

Krystal, H., & Krystal, J. H. (2015). Trauma and affect. In *Integration and Self Healing* (pp. 137-169). Routledge.

Levine, P. A. (2010). *In an unspoken voice: How the body releases trauma and restores goodness*. North Atlantic Books.

McFarlane, A. C. (1992). Avoidance and intrusion in posttraumatic stress disorder. *The Journal of nervous and mental disease, 180*(7), 439-445.

O'Kearney, R., & Perrott, K. (2006). Trauma narratives in posttraumatic stress disorder: A review. *Journal of traumatic stress, 19*(1), 81-93.

Olive, J. (2014). Trauma Representations in Videogames. *work, 2015*, 2015b.

Pederson, J. (2018). Trauma and narrative. *Trauma and literature*, 97-109.

Sar, V., & Ozturk, E. (2013). What is trauma and dissociation?. In *Trauma and Dissociation in a Cross-Cultural Perspective* (pp. 7-20). Routledge.

Sheynin, J., Shind, C., Radell, M., Ebanks-Williams, Y., Gilbertson, M. W., Beck, K. D., & Myers, C. E. (2017). Greater avoidance behavior in individuals with posttraumatic stress disorder symptoms. *Stress, 20*(3), 285-293.

THE REST OF US: HOW QUEER YOUTH FIND THEMSELVES WHEN NO ONE HELPS THEM LOOK

KENNETH SHEPARD

"Older means we're still here." —Frank

In a child's early development years, if they are not taught something or given opportunity to experience it, they often will not learn about it. Some schools do not teach queer history; thus, kids and adolescents may not know what a Pride flag is, what happened at the 1969 Stonewall riots, or who figureheads like Harvey Milk were until their teenage years when they are old enough to seek out that information themselves. Ultimately, educational curriculums and priorities often determine what cultural knowledge kids grow up with. However, this dynamic has shifted dramatically since the internet has become more widely available. Information, ideas, and understanding are at our fingertips, but when these systemic resources disappear, where do queer children turn to learn about who they are and where they come from?

The Last of Us depicts a world in which youths do not have cell phones to search Google for every word, feeling, and skill they do not understand. Instead, they are only taught how to survive where infected, zombie-like creatures roam. If the only culture that survives is what fits in a backpack and or can be found in a long-abandoned building, then culture is just as much a casualty of the apocalypse as anyone who was ever bitten and overtaken by the cordyceps fungus.

 PIECING TOGETHER CULTURE IN THE PIECES LEFT BEHIND

"What's with all the rainbows?" —Dina

Ellie and Lev grow up on different sides of *The Last of Us*'s world, but their self-discovery journeys as queer kids share many parallels — a fact only possible because they come up age in a world without a preserved. Ellie grows up in a Boston quarantine zone, where she attends a military academy that almost exclusively teaches her how to survive in this desolate world, whether by killing infected or members of the Fireflies revolutionary group.

Throughout *The Last of Us*, Ellie's understanding of the world is shown to be incredibly limited. In The *Last of Us: Left Behind* downloadable content (DLC), she explores an abandoned mall with her first love, Riley, and they wonder about the purpose of the stores that are still standing. The apocalypse began in September 2013, and even 20 years later, there is still a Halloween store l filled with masks, props, and toys. Ellie and Riley have never gone trick-or-treating, so when the they wonder aloud about what all this merchandise was for, there was a tacit understanding that kids are not being taught the same lessons or by a traditional education system. They have no context for cultural touchstones that kids their age experienced before the apocalypse leveled society. But Ellie's ignorance regarding the culture of her predecessors goes beyond cultural holidays — it extends to the history of the queer community that came before her.

This theme carries over into *The Last of Us: Part II*. Around five years later, Ellie and her new girlfriend, Dina, stumble into a queer bookstore in Seattle. If the player sticks around long enough, the girls realize that most of the literature left on the store shelves features same-sex pairings, but wonder aloud about "all the rainbows" in reference to the various Pride flags they see hanging on the walls. Even as they stand in a store that was built upon the history of people like them, these young adults do not understand its significance, because no one ever explained it to them.

Ellie's educational failings echo real-world communities without access to scholarly research and information. This might be due to prohibitive costs, lack of access to electricity, and appropriate devices — reasons ultimately rooted in class struggle. When communities lack these resources, they become what Lauren Bradley and Brian Soldo refer to as the "new information poor," referencing how the modern distribution of information through (often costly) digital means affects higher education. If the world of *The Last of Us* does not prioritize the preservation of its own history, it is analogous to that of a modern-day civilization that deprives its citizens of access to proper education. Civilians like Ellie are treated like second-class citizens whose only concern is survival, rather than human beings worthy of enrichment and self-understanding. Instead, she is left to indulge in an imagined nostalgia for an imagined version of the world before, learning more about herself and her worldview through escapism in the form of music, comics, and video games she finds left behind.

While Ellie's ignorance about queer history and identity is due to a systemic failure of public education, Lev's is cultural. He belongs to a Seattle-based cult called the Seraphites, whose worldview is based on the teachings of an unnamed prophet killed by the militaristic Washington Liberation Front (WLF). The group is relatively primitive compared to most established societies in

The Last of Us, only using electricity in specific circumstances, and are gated from outside influence. Their beliefs are centered on nature and living without much of what would be considered civilized by even the post-apocalyptic society. Tools and technology from before the cordyceps fungus leveled the planet are called "old world" and are not allowed in Seraphite society.

This disconnect from the old world, paired with the limited culture that has grown following the outbreak, Lev, his sister Yara, and the rest of the Seraphites have a much different worldview and understanding than even post-apocalypse children have in other communities. They speak English, but when eventual protagonist Abby meets Lev, they have clear language gaps that prevent them from speaking candidly with one another as their friendship blooms. Lev does not know what slang like "cool" means, and when Abby tries to talk to him, there is an obvious difference in how they talk that makes it harder to communicate until they develop rapport.

For Lev, his understanding of his own queer identity as a trans man manifests within a cultural context where t concepts of gender are illustrated to him during childhood. This is similar to someone who realizes their own identity in the context of a heavily monolithic culture, like the conservative Christian communities in the Bible Belt do for rural Americans. Communities that prioritize nuclear family dynamics are likely to cause cognitive dissonance, inner conflict, and isolation in queer youth — and Lev's friction with his own identity and his community is analogous to that of real-world queer youth. If you have ever felt the expectations of a parent's worldview was at odds with what you want, or put you into a box, Lev's story likely rings true to your own lived experience.

In Seraphite culture, gender is visually expressed by one's hairstyle above all else. Women wear their hair as a braided crown, while men shave their heads. When Abby meets Lev and Yara, she learns they are on the run from the Seraphites, and when she asks what they did to be outcasts, Lev meekly says that he shaved his head. Abby, having come from a different upbringing with limited and biased knowledge about Seraphites, believes Lev is lying. However, he is truly communicating what he has done in the only way he knows how, based on his sheltered upbringing. He does not know words like "transgender" or have access to modern gender-affirming care; even so, he expresses his gender identity within his own cultural context.

 HOW FAMILIAL SUPPORT INFORMS QUEER COMFORT AND SELF-CONCEPT

"... but I would like to try." —Ellie

Although Ellie and Lev come from different walks of life within the world of *The Last of Us*, they both still experience different kinds of bigotry and othering, and struggle with how to relate to their peers. Ellie's struggles are a bit subtler, and rooted in that loss of queer culture in the post-apocalypse. Her first experience reckoning with her lesbian identity is in *Left Behind*, in which she has her first kiss with Riley as they confess their feelings for one another. But as we learn in *The Last of Us: Part II* through Ellie's diary entries and a few key scenes, her journey to self-discovery and acceptance was far from over when she and Riley shared this moment.

During *The Last of Us: Part II*'s flashback sequences, Ellie's journal recounts moments of her coming out within her community in Jackson, Wyoming. She gets involved with a girl named Cat, and eventually their relationship becomes an open secret within their friend group. However, Ellie writes that she worries about telling her surrogate father, Joel. Throughout these flashbacks, it is clear Ellie and Joel have become distant since the events of the first game, to the point where Joel seems completely ignorant of Ellie's love life, or her identity as a lesbian.

In a flashback segment two years prior to *The Last of Us: Part II*'s present day, Ellie and Joel are searching for guitar strings while on patrol on the outskirts of Jackson. The dialogue them illustrates a growing distance between the two. Joel attempts to bridge the gap by talking about some of Ellie's interests, but when it comes to Ellie's identity, it is clear the two could not be less aligned.

Joel asks about her friends and personal life as any father would —, and then the topic of Jesse, a male friend in Ellie's group, comes up. As is often the case in any heteronormative society, Joel teases Ellie about the time she spends with Jesse, assuming there's romantic interest. Ellie deflects, but stops short of telling him that she is queer, or that she is dating a woman. Joel's comments may seem innocent enough, but they reaffirm fears Ellie notes in her journal about not knowing whether she should tell Joel about Cat. If Joel assumes by default that Ellie is straight, it sows fear that, if one deviates from the perceived norm, it may result in rejection. Queer children's positive mental health and feelings of belonging can come from several places, whether from their peer groups or through the media they consume, but parental support is also a key factor in self-concept and inward compassion.

The Last of Us: Part II overtly demonstrates that bigotry and heteronormative views are still alive and thriving within places like Jackson, which have a veneer of community covering how toxic viewpoints that are allowed to exist in order to keep the peace. In a flashback to just before the events of the main game, Ellie and Dina share a kiss at a dance in Jackson, and are then confronted by Seth, a drunken bigot who runs a local bar within the town's perimeter. He tells the girls there are kids around and they should not be engaging in such public displays of affection. However, any illusion of simply trying to keep things wholesome goes out the window when he calls Dina a slur, saying it loudly and to the crowd.

The resulting argument illustrates different ways family and community figures handle bigotry. Joel shoves Seth and tells him to "get the hell out" of the dance, while Tommy and Maria (Joel's brother and sister-in-law, and leaders of Jackson's community) attempt to placate Seth and lead him outside so he can get some "fresh air." Joel is intolerant of Seth's intolerance, whereas Maria seems more invested in not letting the fight cause a scene and spoil the evening.

Maria's approach sows more resentment than it makes Ellie feel protected and supported within her community. As is shown in the opening hour of *The Last of Us: Part II*, she forces Ellie to speak with Seth so he can apologize and offer her sandwiches before she goes on patrol, but his phrasing is ambiguous and seemingly insincere. Ellie is unconvinced, but Maria thanks him for his sandwiches and sends Ellie on her way. There is no debrief on what happened, no attempt to make Ellie's feelings heard. She is simply told to move on as if nothing happened.

Meanwhile, Joel's defense of her and Dina finally prompts Ellie to speak to him again after years of distance. They meet up after the dance, and Joel asks if Dina is Ellie's girlfriend. At this point, they are not dating, so Ellie deflects and says it did not mean anything, to which Joel asks more broadly if Ellie likes her. Joel affirms his support, saying that while he does not know Dina's intentions, he believes Dina would be lucky to have Ellie.

Joel and Ellie's relationship is still strained at this point, but this moment of connection allows Ellie to bring down her walls and communicate her anger toward Joel for taking away her agency during *The Last of Us*'s closing hour. They two do not linger on Ellie's coming out, but as it becomes clear she no longer must hide her feelings from Joel, they t can now discuss other matters as their relationship starts to mend.

 QUEER IDENTIFY MANIFESTS
WITHIN AND EVOLVES
AROUND CULTURE

"Only when weak may I carry my true strength." — Lev

Lev's relationship with his mother does not reach the same reconciliation as Ellie's does with Joel. However, it does have parallels in showing how cultures that actively avoid teaching history create rifts between queer children and their peers, parents, and their own selves. Since Lev is not a protagonist in *The Last of Us: Part II*, we do not get a direct line of sight into his mind as we do from Ellie's journal entries, but we learn enough about Seraphite culture to understand how Lev's gender dysphoria manifested within its cultural framework.

As Yara tells Abby, Seraphites have roles within their community that are assigned by elders. While these are not inherently gendered, as Yara is assigned the role of a soldier to fight in the ongoing battle against the Washington Liberation Front, some of them are, such as some young women being assigned to be brides to the elders. Yara explains that Lev had already told her about his feelings of gender dysphoria, but she told him to keep them hidden. However, once he was assigned the role of a wife to one of the elders, Lev shaved his head and announced his new name to the community, resulting in his exile from the Seraphite community.

Lev's defiance of Seraphite teachings in such an explosive manner is the kind of rebellious behavior teenagers use to lash out at tradition, especially the kind that is forced on them against their own beliefs. This interaction taps into a psychological reactivity that arises when one's freedom feels threatened. Lev's trans identity manifests within the cultural framework he has been given. It is clear to the player that Seraphite beliefs are very rigid and views gender in a binary, cis, heteronormative lens. If the Seraphites supported a more fluid understanding of gender and did not confine its people into assigned roles, Lev's transition could have happened within a supportive community. However, the strictness with which certain religious beliefs view the world and limit their followers leads to defiant forms of self-expression.

Despite being exiled and hunted down by those he once considered his community, Lev still maintains that his belief in the teachings of the original Seraphite prophet. He says that the other followers have misrepresented what the belief system initially stood for. This phenomenon is also observed in modern-day religion, including the religious-based reasoning used by Christians to argue against same-sex marriage and gender-affirming care, while others support it based on the same belief system's virtues. Lev's belief in the inherent good of the Seraphites' foundational teachings, which he tells Abby have been misconstrued by his community to further the conflict against the Washington Liberation Front, allows him to still identify as a trans man while maintaining his devotion to his original belief system.

Lev can separate the actions of his community from his religious beliefs, but it is clear he still takes the Seraphites' rejection of him to heart. Because queer people are conditioned to feel a lack of belonging, community becomes paramount to one's own self-concept. Religion is often a tie that binds its followers, placing religious queer people in the difficult situation where their own personal identity results in friction, judgment, or banishment from a communal space.

Lev's belief in and love for his community why he — despite knowing they will likely shoot him on sight — goes to find his mother in their village before leaving Seattle for good. However, when Abby and Yara find him, the confrontation has a tragic end. Lev kills his mother in self-defense, solidifying for him that despite his love of the Seraphite community, they will not accept him if he does not abide by their specific framework.

It is a sad ending, but Lev finds new community with Abby and the Fireflies by the end of *The Last of Us: Part II*. However, this conclusion illustrates a horrifying truth that queer children face when raised in conservative homes. Parents who have an unyielding belief in what their children should be can react poorly, even resorting to the abuse Lev experiences from his mother. Despite this, Lev still shows compassion and love for his mother, even though she has forsaken him for going against the Seraphites' rules and denouncing his assigned role within the cult.

As queer youth often must do when their biological family scorns them, Lev finds a new community with Abby throughout their time together in Seattle. While the Washington Liberation Front's star soldier has trouble communicating with Lev when they first meet, she shows more compassion for Lev's identity and trauma than his own community does, and within just in a few short days of knowing him. When fighting Seraphite forces, Abby hears them call Lev by his dead name, and when he asks if she heard it after the fight, he shows clear signs of distress but asks if Abby wants to talk about it. Rather than prying, Abby asks if Lev wants her to ask about it, which he admits he does not. She drops the conversation, showing respect for Lev's boundaries.

Though she never asks Lev to delve into his trauma, when Yara asks if he and Abby discussed their exile the following day, she asks about the name the Seraphites used. Upon learning the truth of his identity, she expresses compassion, not hatred. It is made explicitly clear Lev has found an ally and surrogate sister, even if the family he grew up with has shunned him. Seth and the Seraphites show that prejudice can survive even a society-leveling pandemic, but Joel and Abby's acceptance and willingness to fight against those who wish Ellie and Lev harm show that safe spaces and unconditional love persist beneath the rubble of a collapsed world.

QUEER PEOPLE HAVE ENDURED
AND SURVIVED

"You're my people." — Abby

Though Ellie and Lev have lived drastically different lives, both of their upbringings, familial relationships, and self-discovery are strong examples of how compassion develops from historical and cultural contexts. Prejudice can manifest in petty ways, like Seth's comments to Ellie and Dina at the dance. It can also be delivered through radical violence, as shown by the Seraphites hunting down Lev for defying their traditions. But prejudice is not the only feeling that takes on these forms. Love, community, and familial connection can also be radical, such as Yara and Abby's defiance of the Seraphites alongside Lev, or it can be much smaller in scale like Joel standing up for Ellie in a crowded Jackson dance.

Ellie and Lev may not know about Pride parades or Stonewall, but they know enough by looking at the communities around them to see that they are different than everybody else. Even as new worldviews sprout up and old ones linger in the post-apocalypse, supporting the people you care about is a universal language spoken by everyone in this world. This remains true even in the absence of a culture or historical record to explain why any of this senseless hatred exists has been lost in collapsed buildings and abandoned bookstores.

As long as queer identity remains othered, support systems are key to young LGBTQIA+ kids feeling comfortable being themselves. Ellie found belonging in her friends in Jackson, but Joel's assumptions about her sowed a feeling of anxiety in their relationship. Lev stood against the expectations of his people, and in doing so found a new, supportive community where he could be himself. Ellie and Lev may not have access to the education that would give them words and definitions for everything they feel, and the fights it took to get those terms in dictionaries — but thanks to the support of their found families, perhaps they can come up with new terms and build new histories even in this post-apocalyptic world.

About the Author

KENNETH SHEPARD is a New York-based journalist and critic seen on sites like Kotaku, Fanbyte, IGN, Polygon, Gayming Magazine, and others in the video game space. His coverage of The Last of Us Part II at Fanbyte, covering topics of grief, queerness, and player agency, was nominated for Best Ongoing Coverage by Good Games Writing. He has since covered the Max live-action series and franchise at Kotaku, and a 16-episode podcast retrospective on both games for Normandy FM. He also spent an absurd amount of money to buy the officially licensed replica of Ellie's guitar during the height of the COVID-19 pandemic.

References

Bradley, L. & Soldo, B. (2011) The New Information Poor: How Limited Access to Digital Scholarly Resources Impacts Higher Education, The Serials Librarian, 61:3-4, 366-376, DOI: 10.1080/0361526X.2011.592667

Ford, D. (2021). The Salve and the Sting of Religion/Spirituality in Queer and Transgender BIPOC. In: Nadal, K.L., Scharrón-del Río, M.R. (eds) Queer Psychology. Springer, Cham. https://doi.org/10.1007/978-3-030-74146-4_15

Hatchel, T., Merrin, G., Espelage, D. (2019) Peer victimization and suicidality among LGBTQ youth: the roles of school belonging, self-compassion, and parental support, Journal of LGBT Youth, 16:2, 134-156, DOI: 10.1080/19361653.2018.1543036

Koltko-Rivera, M. (2004). The Psychology of Worldviews. Review of General Psychology. http://www.arabphilosophers.com/Arabic/aresearch/anon-arabic/anonarabic%20research/Worldview/Mark%20E.%20Koltko-Rivera/the_psychology_of_worldviews.pdf.

Van Petegem S, Soenens B, Vansteenkiste M, Beyers W. Rebels with a cause? Adolescent defiance from the perspective of reactance theory and self-determination theory. Child Dev. 2015 May-Jun;86(3):903-18. doi: 10.1111/cdev.12355. Epub 2015 Feb 23. PMID: 25702962.

Wulf, T., Breuer, J. S., & Schmitt, J. B. (2022). Escaping the pandemic present: The relationship between nostalgic media use, escapism, and well-being during the COVID-19 pandemic. Psychology of Popular Media, 11(3), 258–265. https://doi.org/10.1037/ppm0000357

BILL AND FRANK ENDURED SO BILL AND FRANK COULD LOVE

CHARALAMBOS "HARRY" LOIZIDES

"You Were My Purpose." —Bill

The Last of Us, a generation-defining video game, masterfully weaves a compelling story of the human condition decades after a worldwide infectious outbreak leaves chaos in its wake. Amidst powerful environmental storytelling, we are introduced to complex main characters and subtler side characters. A decade later, HBO's TV series *The Last of Us* attempted (and succeeded) in crafting its own interpretation of the decimated world and the multi-shaded characters within it.

In particular, the story of side characters Bill and Frank shines through and provides a lasting impact for players of the game and viewers of the show. In *The Last of Us* video game, we see the postscript of a relationship — weathered down by years of friction that eventually devolves into animosity. In contrast, *The Last of Us* show offers a powerful arc of these queer partners' lives together — from start, to peak, to end. The massive shift in story from video game to live action may have surprised some fans. However, the societal shift between releases offered time for this once tepid story to grow into its own contained queer love saga.

MEDIA'S PORTRAYAL OF LGBTQ+ CHARACTERS

The media portrayal of LGBTQ+ individuals has evolved significantly over the years, reflecting changing societal attitudes and a growing awareness of the diversity within the LGBTQ+ community. Historically, representation of these characters in media has been limited, and often characterized by stereotypes and negative tropes.

As societal attitudes towards LGBTQ+ issues began to evolve, so did their media representation. The late 20th century saw an increase in queer visibility, with some shows and films featuring such characters in more prominent roles. However, many of these representations were still limited by narrow, often negative, and sensationalized narratives — perpetuating stereotypes and contributing to the marginalization of the LGBTQ+ community.

In more recent years, there has been a marked improvement in the media's approach to LGBTQ+ representation. Filmmakers and showrunners are increasingly recognizing the importance of authentic storytelling that goes beyond clichés and tropes. This shift is evident in projects like *The Last of Us*, a critically acclaimed video game that addresses LGBTQ+ themes through its characters, Frank and Bill.

Frank and Bill's storyline in *The Last of Us* stands out for its thoughtful exploration of LGBTQ+ identity within the context of a post-apocalyptic world. Their relationship is portrayed with depth and sensitivity, avoiding common pitfalls of tokenism or sensationalism. The characters are defined by more than just their sexual orientation; they are complex individuals with unique personalities, motivations, and struggles.

The Last of Us received praise for its commitment to inclusivity and for treating its several LGBTQ+ characters with the same narrative weight as their heterosexual counterparts. This approach reflects a broader trend in media, where creators increasingly recognize the importance of diverse and authentic representation. The inclusion of well-developed LGBTQ+ characters contributes to a more inclusive and empathetic media landscape, fostering understanding and acceptance.

While progress has been made, challenges continue to persist. LGBTQ+ representation in media does not yet fully reflect the diversity within the community, and there is still work to be done to ensure that stories are told with nuance and authenticity. Additionally, the impact of media representation extends beyond individual characters; it also creates inclusive environments behind the scenes, with diverse voices shaping the narratives.

 "I HAD SOMEBODY THAT I CARED ABOUT." —THE STORY OF BILL & FRANK IN THE VIDEO GAME

In the context of the progressive social growth over the past several years, it is valuable to understand how the story of Bill and Frank emerged in Naughty Dog's video game interpretation of *The Last of Us*.

Several hours into the game, we come upon the small town of Lincoln, Massachusetts. Joel, a rugged older gentleman, has been tasked to escort an angsty teenager, Ellie, across the country in hopes of stopping this infestation pandemic once and for all. While cautiously entering the town, Joel explains to Ellie, "Bill ain't exactly the most... stable of individuals. So, when we get there, you let me do the talkin'." Before even encountering this new character, players are already predisposed to having a negative portrayal of Bill — reminiscent of other negative depictions of LGBTQ+ characters in media at the time. Whether intentional or not, the subtle hostility towards this character is established, regardless of how he will react in the story.

Eventually, with all the fortification around town, Joel is snared in a trap and Ellie is forced to rescue him. Throughout this ordeal, a pack of infected begin to bombard the duo, ultimately getting rescued by Bill — the strange survivor that Joel had previous dealings with, and toward whom the player already has trepidations. After dealing with the infected, Bill's paranoia forces him to subdue Ellie and Joel, in fear that they may be infected. Following a heated few moments, Bill agrees to help the two procure a car to continue their journey.

Shortly after, Bill provides a bit of additional context from his past. In a short, in-game cinematic clip, Bill begins with:

Let me tell you a story. Once upon a time I had somebody I cared about. [pause] It was a partner. Somebody I had to look after.

In this instant, the frantic, highly cautious character washes away and a broken heart emerges from that blip of a pause. The emotional weight of identifying a partner created for Bill immense hardship and pain in that brief moment. Players with a keen eye can see that this is something worth noting — a moment in time that provides powerful allusions to Bill's past and may contextualize Bill's current state.

However, the sharp-tempered Bill we first met quickly returns and continues his story:

And in this world that sort of shit is good for one thing. Gettin' ya killed. So you know what I did? I wised the fuck up. And I realized it's gotta be just me.

The second half of this quote significantly turns the joy of having a partner into the pain of losing one. In this moment it is not clear whether Bill's partner voluntarily left or was forced away, but the emotional pain that Bill still holds onto is layered and raw. In either instance, Bill has a difficult time reconciling his emotions about this break with his partner. For now, Bill is forced to compartmentalize his emotions and focus on his safety and security as he helps Joel and Ellie find a car battery so they can continue their journey.

After a failed attempt to find that car battery, Joel and Bill get into a heated and escalated argument. Inside a random house in town, the two men throw insults at one another and, once again, Bill is hit by an emotional ton of bricks. Bill, at this moment, lingers his eyes towards a hanging corpse. Still in a heated fit, the dialogue continues:

Joel: *What? Do you know this guy or something?*

Bill: *Frank.*

Joel: *Who the hell's Frank?*

Bill: *He was my partner. [Bill pauses, then walks towards the hanging corpse]*

Bill: *He was the only idiot that would wear a shirt like that.* [Bill then cuts Frank's body down]

Bill: *He's got bites. Here and...*

Joel: *I reckon he didn't want to turn so he...*

Bill: *Yeah, I guess not. Well, fuck him.*

Like the first interaction mentioned in this section, Bill's entire demeanor changes. His emotional vulnerability is visible, the pain in his eyes is palpable, and his stammering demonstrates that he is moments away from a breakdown. To cope, Bill then slings off an insult towards Frank in hopes of refocusing toward the current predicament instead of self-reflecting on his emotional weight and grief.

Moments later, we find out that Frank had already found the car battery, and even prepped it into a car in hopes of escaping Lincoln. In a last-ditch effort to prepare for the final leg of this arc, players stumble onto a letter that Frank wrote for Bill in his final moments.

> *Well, Bill, I doubt you'd ever find this note 'cause you were too scared to ever make it to this part of town. But if for some reason you did, I want you to know I hated your guts. I grew tired of this shitty town and your set-in-your-ways attitude. I wanted more from life than this and you could never get that.*
>
> *And that stupid battery you kept moaning about — I got it. But I guess you were right. Trying to leave this town will kill me. Still better than spending another day with you.*
>
> *Good Luck,*
>
> *Frank*

Frank, still full of frustration and pain, attempts to put in as many hurtful comments in his last letter as he could. Each comment is more damaging than the last, but he ultimately wishes Bill good luck as a parting farewell. That final line, which could be interpreted as a simple salutation, also suggests Frank's subconscious emotions. Despite all the horribly sharp comments, he truly wishes the best for Bill and that Bill can ultimately find more in life, like Frank wanted.

Bill, when confronted with this letter, breathe deeply and reiterates some hurtful comments about Frank, and is quick to deflect and ask Joel if he is ready to depart. After successfully restarting the car and leaving the town of Lincoln, Ellie discloses that she pilfered a few reading materials from Bill. Ellie specifically mentions a gay adult magazine, which confirms Bill's sexual orientation that had to that point only been alluded to throughout this story arc in the game.

Ultimately, Bill and Frank's subtle story devolved from the weight of this world. A relationship where the two men seem to have deeply cared for each other at one point, until a volatile breakup left them both angry, bitter, and alone. This somber end to their relationship seems to harken back to the negative and hostile tropes of the past, implying that this deviant behavior is meant to end in suffering for all parties involved.

However, ten years later, the TV release of HBO's *The Last of Us* series opted to evolve the narrative of Bill and Frank into an emotional pillar for LGBTQ+ stories.

"ENDURE AND SURVIVE." — THE DECADE OF SOCIETAL GROWTH

Bridging the timeframe between the original release of the game and the series premiere of the show, *The Last of Us* presented a powerful microcosm of how society transformed through those years with an LGBTQ+ lens.

Various Gallup Polls indicate that in 1996, only 27% of the people polled believed that marriages between same-sex couples should be legally recognized, while 68% believed that these marriages should not be valid. In 2013, the year the game was released and same-sex marriage was legalized in the United States, the percentage nearly doubled (53%) in support of same-sex marriage, with 45% of the people surveyed stating that they were opposed.

In 2023, the year the HBO show released, the trend continued and 71% of surveyors stated that marriages between same-sex couples should be valid, while only 28% stated that these marriages should not be valid. Over those 27 years, the gap between opposing opinions not only widened even greater, but actually reversed within the public opinion.

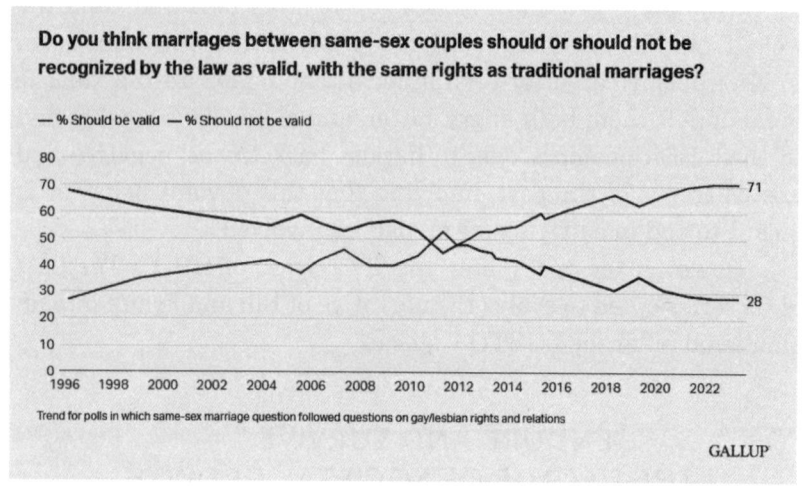

Graph 1

In addition to changing societal beliefs, there is now greater media representation, including more meaningful LGBTQ+ characters. A study in 2015 concluded there is a positive correlation between exposure to on-screen gay characters and pro-LGBTQ+ beliefs. Another study demonstrated that the media experienced by gay, lesbian, and bisexual people influenced their self-realization, coming out, and current identities, while also providing a source of pride, inspiration, and comfort.

The Gay & Lesbian Alliance Against Defamation (GLAAD), also quantifiably tracks these trends in yearly summary reports titled "Where We Are on TV." In the 2012-2013 calendar year, across primetime scripted television programs on the five broadcast networks (ABC, CBS, The CW, Fox, and NBC), 31 characters are LGBTQ+. In the 2022-2023 calendar year, across all platforms (including primetime broadcast, primetime scripted cable, and major streaming services), there are 596 LGBTQ+ characters. With an over 1800% increase in comparison between the 2012-2013 and 2022-2023 calendar years, visibility has skyrocketed unprecedented levels.

These different forms of media have provided more safe havens for LGBTQ+ people seeking avenues of relevance and representation for others to understand and accept. This visibility reflects a concept known as social learning theory, which maintains that people acquire knowledge and new behaviors by observing and imitating others. Albert Bandura, the psychologist who coined the theory, states:

...most human behavior is learned observationally through modeling: from observing others one forms an idea of how new behaviors are performed, and on later occasions, this coded information serves as a guide for action.

For many queer people, finding the right words or expressions to describe themselves or how they feel is far too foreign. That is, until new vocabulary, new stories, and new experiences are presented to them. Places where LGBTQ+ people once felt unseen now offer opportunity for self-realization, thanks to the models presented in an ever-increasing and nuanced form of media.

"I THINK I'M GONNA LOVE YOU FOR A LONG, LONG TIME." —THE STORY OF BILL AND FRANK IN LIVE ACTION

This more nuanced is further showcased by HBO's *The Last of Us* series. Though much of the show is drawn directly from the video game, the HBO series decides to take a bold, intimate pivot towards the story of Bill and Frank.

In this episode, we see Bill — literally and metaphorically — build a wall in the surrounding area of his home, located in a small town abandoned days after the initial outbreak of the pandemic. As a well-prepared survivalist, Bill begins fortifying his defenses and organizing his resources to best live out his life, not unlike Maslow's base level in his hierarchy of needs. With his immediate needs now met, Bill begins to live safely. However, he does not progress his life beyond simply surviving. His base needs of safety and physicality are met, and he is portrayed as "content enough" for years on end. Bill, rigid as ever, finds solace in his routine — performing the same operations, security checks, and maintenance to ensure his survival. The only moments we see of Bill showing any animated emotions are when his defensive perimeter traps ensnare an infected creature.

This all changed, however, when a non-infected random man fell for one of Bill's perimeter traps. Bill, still overly cautious and defensive of his property and safety, has concerns about the man he trapped. Frank, the one caught in the trap, attempts to make jokes, and we see a sincerity towards Bill emerge. Eventually, Bill offers Frank an opportunity to shower, some new clothes, and a warm meal. Still, Bill is primarily concerned about his safety, while Frank is overly appreciative and compassionate towards him. To break the ice further, Frank points to the piano and begins playing Linda Ronstadt's "Long, Long Time." After a few moments of

Frank performing the song, Bill offers some mildly rude comments about Frank's loud and boisterous rendition. In a sassy, yet whimsical manner, Frank invites Bill to perform the song instead. Melodically, Bill performs the song, where each keystroke and note is purposeful and passionate. He quietly finishes and pulls away from the piano.

This is the first time Bill is shows vulnerability in the show, well beyond his safety concerns and physical well-being. We witness powerful character development when Bill lowers his emotional wall, which he erected several years prior (and likely many years before the outbreak even began). The emotional tension between Bill and Frank continues, where Frank asks, "So who's the girl? Girl you're singing about?" Eyes red and full of tears, Bill responds, "There is no girl." Frank says, "I know," leans in, and they share a tender and emotional kiss.

With all this buildup, the show allows the viewers to see the escalation in subtle, yet powerful cues that led to this moment. Overly done tropes or stereotypes for LGBTQ+ characters were thrown out the window. Instead, Nick Offerman and Murray Bartlett, who played Bill and Frank, respectively, delved deep in their acting knowledge to showcase the love between these two characters. A lingering look, a brush of hair covering the face, and even a smirk in a witty comment, helped thread the details that allowed the characters to shine through and resonate so profoundly with current viewership.

If an attempt at portraying this moment was done in the early 2010s, Hollywood likely would have muted much of its impact and opted for a more abrasive dynamic, echoing the video game. Instead of offering the groundwork to a wholesome love, it may have been portrayed as the forbidden fruit that no one should have, but secretly desire. Despite this, the 2023 rendition put forth an authentic and vulnerable start to a relationship, gripping the audience in hopes of seeing more.

From here, the dynamic between Bill and Frank grew exponentially, while also seeing some natural ebbs and flows. Instead of arguing about money, they bicker about their "allocation of resources." Bill, whose new personal mission is to keep Frank safe, is actively challenged for the first time in years. Instead of just being safe, Frank exclaims, "Our home isn't just our house, it's everything around us." But before Bill is able to offer a rebuttal, Frank interrupts, "If you say 'resource management,' so help me, I will run through one of your trip wires."

The experience of bickering with a partner is instantaneously relatable to anyone in a relationship, regardless of who the relationship is with. Including this moment in the series only allows viewers see Bill and Frank as more than simply a token same-sex couple, but rather a template for couples of any iteration finding a path towards growth and love; a milestone we likely would not have seen without the societal growth over the past decade. Even the fact that Bill agrees to Frank's request shows that the two are pushing each other towards a better and more fulfilling life. Characters that were once treated as one-dimensional in the video game grew into TV characters who were instead multi-layered in their depth, motivation, and goals.

"PAYING ATTENTION TO THINGS, IT'S HOW WE SHOW LOVE."

Even after this small victory, Frank cannot help himself and declares that the two are finally going to have friends. Frank continues to push Bill out of his comfort zone and even invites people that he has met virtually over for lunch. Bill, resistant as ever towards change, casually holds his gun directed at the guests, who we know as Joel and Tess. The small quibbles between Bill and Frank continue to showcase their individually poignant perspectives. Bill is cautious as ever, while Frank lovingly attempts to elevate their lives towards a life worth living. In this brief glimpse, we forget about the apocalypse and just see four adults sharing a meal on a beautiful day.

Years go by once again, and we see Bill and Frank continuing to live their lives. To stay healthy, the two are encourage each other to finish a run, a situation any couple could see themselves in. Towards the end of their workout, Frank surprises Bill with a patch of strawberries, a rarity in this world. They share a touching moment, showcasing their love, and Bill, somber in the moment, apologies for getting older faster than Frank. Lovingly, Frank replies, "I like you older. Older means we're still here."

Ten years later, the two characters are in their late stage of life. Frank, now suffering from a debilitating disease, is unable to walk and confined to a wheelchair. They still enjoy each other's company, both living out their lives with creative outlets such as painting and gardening. Even the occasional wink towards each other, though subtle, show the deep affection for one another. The mundane act of remembering pills, though heartbreaking, is another touchstone with older couples who have been through a lot, but in their hearts, want to be there for each other.

Eventually, Frank declares to Bill that that day would be his last. Visibly upset, Bill stumbles on his words with questions and hope of a cure in the near future. Instead, Frank asks Bill "for one more good day" where the two get married, and eventually "fall asleep in your arms." Since the show's apocalyptic event occurred in the early 1990s, same-sex marriage was not legal. Allowing these two to declare their love, articulate their vows, and exchange their rings was a powerful moment. Despite any societal obstacles from their past, these characters fulfill their dream, and the show celebrates for their love.

Ultimately, Bill and Frank decide to pass away in their sleep after ingesting enough pills in the same wine that they first shared together 16 years prior.

 "LET ME LOVE YOU THE WAY I WANT"

The evolution of Bill and Frank transcends the typical love story. They find each other under trying circumstances, with both cautious of each other at first. The trepidation quickly turns to compassion, and they form a wonderful relationship over a delicious meal and melodic music. The love between two men, once taboo, became the centerpiece of a decades-long paradigm shift of societal psychological trends, political discussions, and media portrayal.

Love is love. And with that love, society continues to thrive in its journey towards seeing that love in all its glory. What was once a subtle relationship in a prestige video game in 2013, became a prominent storyline for a major drama series a decade later.

Regardless of who you love, *The Last of Us* gives society a template for representing the emotional weight of the love between two people who deserve it.

"From an objective point of view, it's incredibly romantic." —Frank

About the Author

CHARALAMBOS "HARRY" LOIZIDES is an award-winning secondary mathematics teacher in Long Island, New York with a decade of experience in the field. He encourages students to grow through their academic experiences and develop their skills both in and out of the classroom. With this, Mr. Loizides continues to find meaningful and dynamic ways to blend mathematical topics with numerous video and tabletop games. He has previously presented on these topics at Educator's Day at New York Comic Con, PAX East, PAX West, PAX Unplugged, as well as several education-based conferences like the Long Island Mathematics Conference and Association of Teachers of Mathematics of New York City Annual Conference. Mr. Loizides is also the Editor-in-Chief of Six One Indie, an independently operated games media outlet with a focus on amplifying the voices of indie games and developers.

References:

Bandura, A. (1977). Social learning theory. Englewood Cliffs, NJ: Prentice Hall.

Bond, B. J., & Compton, B. L. (2015, November 30). Gay on-screen: The relationship between exposure to gay characters on television and heterosexual audiences' endorsement of Gay Equality. *Journal of Broadcasting &; Electronic Media*, 59(4), 717–732. https://doi.org/10.1080/08838151.2015.1093485

Gallup. (2023, July 6). *LGBTQ+ rights*. Gallup.com. https://news.gallup.com/poll/1651/gay-lesbian-rights.aspx

Gomillion, S. C., & Giuliano, T. A. (2011, February 25). The influence of media role models on gay, lesbian, and bisexual identity. *Journal of Homosexuality*, 58(3), 330–354. https://doi.org/10.1080/00918369.2011.546729

Hire, R.O. 2007. An interview with Frank Rundle, MD. In American Psychiatry and Homosexuality: An Oral History, ed. J. Drescher, J.P. Merlino, 115-130. New York: Harrington Park Press.

Linda Ronstadt. (1970). Long, long time. Elliot Mazer.

Maslow, Abraham H. (1943). "A theory of human motivation". Psychological Review. 50 (4): 370–396. CiteSeerX 10.1.1.334.7586. doi:10.1037/h0054346. hdl:10983/23610. ISSN 0033-295X. OCLC 1318836

Mazin, C., Spence, G., & O'Connor, C. (2023, January 29). Long, Long Time. *The Last of Us*. episode 3, New York, New York; HBO.

McCarthy, J. (2022, May 12). *Gallup first polled on gay issues in '77. What has changed?* Gallup.com. https://news.gallup.com/poll/258065/gallup-first-polled-gay-issues-changed.aspx

Naughty Dog. (2013). *The Last of Us* [PlayStation 3]. Sony Computer Entertainment.

The Last of Us Wiki (2024). The Last of Us Bill's Town. Retrieved from https://thelastofus.fandom.com/wiki/Bill%27s_Town

Tucker, B. (2023, November 29). *Representation in the media of LGBTQ+*. SeatUp, LLC. https://seatup.com/blog/lgbtq-representation-in-the-media/

van Meer, M. M., & Pollmann, M. M. (2021, September 22). Media representations of lesbians, gay men, and bisexuals on Dutch television and people's stereotypes and attitudes about LGBs. *Sexuality & Culture, 26*(2), 640–664. https://doi.org/10.1007/s12119-021-09913-x

THE LOSS OF US: A PSYCHOANALYTIC VIEW OF LOSS AND LOVE IN THE LAST OF US GAMES

ANGELO MIRRA

"I struggled for a long time with surviving. And, no matter what, you keep finding something to fight for." —Joel

 INTRODUCTION

The Last of Us stands as a transformative narrative that has sparked extensive discussions since its debut. Unlike many other video games, its remarkable narrative strength is deeply rooted in the human experience, making it a symbolic journey for players. Through the intertwined stories of Joel, Ellie, Abby, and other characters, the game takes players on a profound exploration of emotions and experiences. It unveils the dark facets of humanity, portraying individuals reduced to violent animals, while also highlighting the enduring power of love in the face of a desolate world.

Joel embodies a poignant archetype — a father who, after losing his daughter, transforms into a monstrous figure driven not by revenge but by a profound loss of faith in others and himself, a psychological state known as dissociation. His sole motivation becomes survival in this harsh reality.

What most sets *The Last of Us* apart is its unique ability to serve as a mirror for players, reflecting aspects of themselves through the characters of Ellie, Abby, and particularly Joel. These characters become prototypes through which players can vicariously experience the complex emotions of being a son, a father, a murderer, a victim, and more — while exploring their own identities through themes of love and personal loss.

 ECHOES OF THE PSYCHE: MOURNING AND MELANCHOLIA IN *THE LAST OF US*

What drives a devoted father and a decent man to become heartless? By stripping him of everything he holds dear, shattering his universe and his entire existence.

Joel, a carpenter from Austin, Texas, shares his life with his brother, Tommy, and his daughter, Sarah, whose mother remains unmentioned and unseen throughout the game. Their peaceful existence is shattered when, on Joel's birthday, they are forced to flee due to the rapid spread of a deadly cordyceps fungus, for which there appears to be no cure. In their desperate attempt to escape the ensuing chaos, Sarah injures her leg and is fatally shot by a soldier attempting to prevent their escape. Joel's futile efforts to save Sarah end in a heart-wrenching scene of him cradling his deceased daughter, setting the tone for the game's sorrowful narrative.

Society as we know it has collapsed, and Joel now resides in Boston, one of the remaining cities. Working in exchange for food rations and engaging in illicit smuggling with his partner, Tess,

Joel is haunted by nightmares of Sarah's death, even twenty years later. This event has transformed Joel into a man who is utterly ruthless, withdrawn, and mistrustful of others.

Psychoanalytic theories suggest that humans are driven by two primary forces: hunger and love, representing the instincts for self-preservation and sexuality. These are considered the core of our daily emotional expressions. Freud further categorized these into life drives — associated with love and creativity towards life and pleasure — and death drives, which are destructive forces leading to loss and death. In *The Last of Us*, survival instincts predominate, with aggression and survival tactics becoming a fundamental aspect of this new, harsh reality.

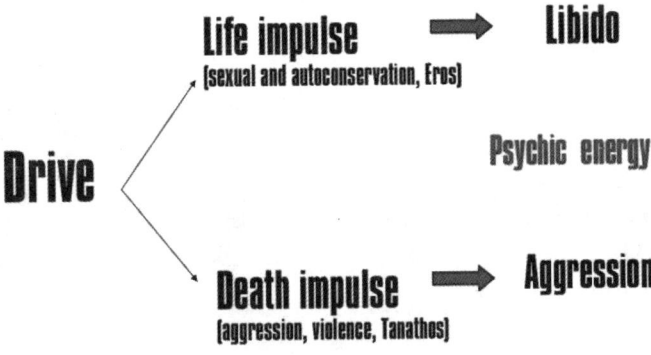

Figure 1

The narrative of the game is anchored in the primal instinct for survival, with Joel profoundly affected by his daughter's death, leading to a life of sorrow, fixated on that pivotal moment. He emerges as a detached, cynical, and ruthless individual, driven solely by the desire to persevere, indifferent to any consequences. Joel's complete emotional detachment stems from his perpetual suffering, characterized by the void left by Sarah. His antagonism is fueled by a deep-seated resentment and jealousy of a world that robbed him of his child.

It is revealed that Joel contemplated suicide in the two decades between the game's prologue and its main storyline, feeling devoid of purpose after losing Sarah. However, failing to end his life, he finds the strength to continue, redirecting his bitterness and anger towards others, rather than himself. This psychological mechanism is straightforward: to shield the ego from intolerable reality by outwardly projecting all distressing emotions and sensations, convincing the psyche that the source of negativity lies outside the self.

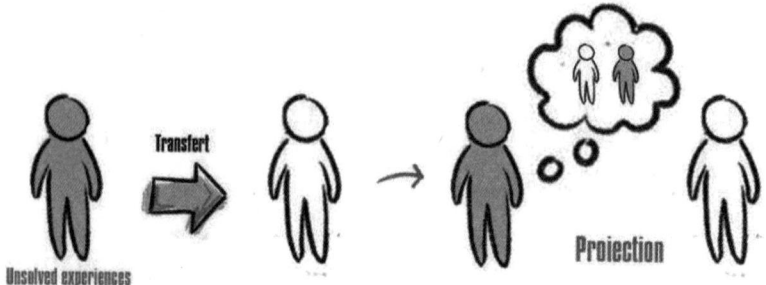

Figure 2

Hatred and aversion are closely related emotions. Hatred suppresses empathy and positive feelings, perpetuating Joel's internal divide and enabling his cold and cynical demeanor. On the other hand, aversion reflects his inner turmoil, manifesting resistance to any form of human connection.

Ellie represents the key to reawakening love within Joel. Initially, he meets her with the same mistrust he shows everyone, but his sense of duty gradually rekindles his paternal instincts, paving the way for his transformation. Despite Joel's initial resistance and his tendency to see Ellie as a surrogate for Sarah, their relationship evolves, lowering his defenses and fostering empathy for someone he comes to view not just as a responsibility but as a genuine connection. Ellie's presence in Joel's life allows him to confront his vulnerabilities and rediscover the capacity to love. Joel finds redemption in protecting Ellie, as she, in turn, saves him.

 AFFECTION AND ANXIETY: THE DYNAMICS OF EROS AND THANATOS IN *THE LAST OF US*

Joel's routine is disrupted when Tess brings him into a deal with the Fireflies, a rebel group opposing the authoritative government and its martial law. Marlene, the leader of the Fireflies, offers them a mission to transport a young girl, Ellie, from Boston to a research facility at the University of Eastern Colorado, promising weapons and a vehicle as payment—a vehicle Joel needs to reunite with his brother in Wyoming. The mission's purpose is initially unclear to Joel and Tess, and they are indifferent to the details as long as they receive their compensation. However, they soon discover Ellie's secret: she is immune to the infection that has ravaged humanity, and her immunity could be key to developing a cure.

This revelation comes as they are forced out of safety and pursued by infected creatures known as clickers. Tragically, Tess is bitten and infected. In her final moments, Tess reveals her infection to Joel, contrasting it with Ellie's immunity, and implores him to see the truth of their situation. She extracts a promise from Joel to deliver Ellie to the Fireflies, seeking redemption through this final request. Despite his deep sorrow, Joel commits to fulfilling Tess's dying wish.

This opening narrative sets up a stark contrast: Joel, initially indifferent to Ellie and her unique condition, and Tess, who, facing her imminent transformation into one of the infected, chooses to entrust Joel with a significant responsibility. Tess's sacrifice and Joel's subsequent commitment mark the beginning of his transformation.

The dynamics at play involve Joel grappling with his conscience and Tess seeking to mend her self-image before her death. Tess leverages Joel's sense of guilt, convincing him to take on the mission despite his initial resistance and self-perception as merely a survivor, not a villain. Ellie, an orphan accustomed to being used and abandoned, reluctantly accepts Joel's protection, which, to her surprise, includes genuine care. This unexpected act of kindness begins to forge a bond between them. Joel embodies the harsh realities of human nature, while Ellie represents the lost innocence of childhood marred by suffering. Their relationship bridges the gaps in their experiences, drawing them closer.

Throughout their journey, Joel and Ellie meet various characters who exemplify themes of loss and control. One such character is Bill, who lives in seclusion following his partner's suicide. Despite Joel's choice to keep his own pain private to spare Bill further pain, this approach inadvertently causes more suffering for them both. Bill mirrors an aspect of Joel's past self: experiencing the loss of a loved one, yet continuing to live with an openness to others instead of shutting himself off completely.

Other poignant examples are brothers Sam and Henry, whose tragic fates deeply affect Joel and intensify his resolve to safeguard Ellie. The tragedy unfolds as Sam, infected and turning into a clicker, is killed by Henry in self-defense. Overwhelmed by guilt, Henry then takes his own life. These encounters profoundly influence Joel, particularly reflecting his own immense fear of loss. This experience leads to a gradual softening of Joel's tough exterior, as he learns to embrace his growing attachment to Ellie.

The narrative peaks in Wyoming, where Joel's meeting with his brother Tommy confronts him with his past and the fear of failing Ellie as he did his daughter. Ellie's fear of abandonment leads her to run away, setting the stage for a pivotal moment between her and Joel. Their confrontation represents the culmination of their journey's emotional and psychological challenges, highlighting the transformation in their relationship and individual growth:

Joel: *You realize how much your life is worth, huh? Running away like that, putting yourself in danger, are stupid gestures.* Ellie: *Then I would say the disappointment is mutual .*Joel: *What do you want from me?* Ellie: *Admit that you've been trying to get rid of me since the beginning.*[...]

Ellie: *I'm not her, you know?*

Joel: *What?*

Ellie: *Maria told me about Sarah and I...*

Joel: *Ellie! You're playing with fire: be careful what you say.*

Ellie: *I'm sorry for your daughter Joel, but I've lost someone too.*

Joel: *You have no idea what that means.*

Ellie: *Everyone I loved has died or left me. Everybody! Except fucking you! And don't tell me I'd be safer with someone else, because the truth is, I'd just be more afraid.*

Joel: *You're right. You are not my daughter and I am not your father. And everyone will go their own way.*

In this pivotal moment, Ellie profoundly impacts Joel, breaching his emotional barriers with genuine empathy. Melanie Klein discusses this phenomenon as the introduction of psychological "ghosts" into another person, aiming to harm, dominate, or control them. Joel shields himself from grief by casting the shadow of Sarah onto Ellie, seeing her as the embodiment of his projections. Conversely, Ellie challenges Joel by compelling him to confront reality. This mutual dependency completes the formation of their bond. Joel begins to truly empathize with someone else, recognizing that his new purpose extends beyond mere survival to protecting Ellie.

However, the narrative reintroduces the theme of loss as Joel, driven by a fierce love, confronts the Fireflies to prevent Ellie's surgery. Although sacrificing Ellie could potentially benefit humanity by leading to a cure for the cordyceps infection, for Joel, it would mean enduring another profound loss. The story concludes ambiguously, leaving it uncertain whether Ellie's sacrifice would indeed save humanity, thus sparking a personal reflection for the player. This open-ended conclusion invites players to weigh their own moral values against their emotional journey with the characters.

The game masterfully intertwines emotions such as fear, hatred, loss, love, guilt, joy, and envy, urging players to ponder a critical question: *What would I have done?* This deep emotional engagement with Joel and Ellie's story encourages players to reflect on their own values and decisions, embodying the game's central themes.

FROM ENMITY TO HEALING: THE PSYCHOANALYTIC JOURNEY OF HATE AND REPARATION IN *THE LAST OF US*

Following the narrative established in the first part of the game, the sequel delves into themes of hatred, loss, and their ties to the pursuit of revenge. Revenge is portrayed as an attempt to compensate for anguish endured by the characters, seeking to restore balance for what was unjustly taken. The intention of the narrative is not to coerce the player into aligning with either Ellie or Abby, but to challenge them to empathize and reconsider their perspectives. The core message here addresses the cyclical nature of violence, highlighting its endless capacity to inflict pain, erode the human spirit, and lead to self-destruction. Efforts to rectify past wrongs through anger and vengeance only perpetuate a cycle of suffering, entrapping both the victim and the perpetrator in a relentless spiral of death and retribution. This cycle is manifested in the game through Ellie and Abby's thirst for revenge, illustrating how their actions echo and amplify their pain, leaving no room for clear-cut heroes or villains. In their respective narratives, Ellie and Abby mirror each other across different contexts and backstories, emphasizing the universality of their experiences.

In the sequel, Ellie's journey becomes a focal point. We see her increasingly isolated from Joel, who assumes the role of a repentant father figure, softened by his life with Ellie and the semblance of normalcy they found. However, Joel's deception about the Fireflies and the events at the hospital triggers in Ellie a profound identity crisis and sense of betrayal. Her anger towards Joel is rooted in self-guilt for seemingly dooming humanity and her frustration over being denied agency. Despite her struggle to process her grief and move towards forgiveness, this internal battle comes to the forefront during a pivotal flashback, where Ellie and Joel confront the truths and lies that have shaped their relationship.

> Ellie: *I should have died in that hospital. My life would have made fucking sense. But you prevented me from doing so.*
>
> Joel: *If the Lord would allow me to relive that day... I would do it again. I would do the same again.*
>
> Ellie: *Yes... It's that... I don't think I'll ever forgive you. But I'd like to give it a try.*
>
> Joel: *I hope so.*

Unknown to Ellie (and the player), setting the stage for the unfolding drama, is another young woman seeking vengeance for her father's death. This woman, Abby, the daughter of the chief surgeon of the Fireflies, aims to avenge her father, who was killed by Joel while he rescued Ellie from the hospital. Abby's quest for revenge is driven by a narrative she is unaware of: Joel's reasons for his actions and Ellie's perspective on the matter. The crux of the game revolves around this tragic cycle of violence and revenge.

When Abby takes Joel's life in front of Ellie, it is not just an act of retribution, but a reopening of Ellie's wounds from past losses—her mother, her friend Riley, and now Joel. This ignites a fierce desire in Ellie for vengeance against Abby, marking a dark path where Ellie sees in her victims a reflection of her unresolved feelings towards Joel. His death triggers in Ellie a cascade of traumatic stress, haunted by recurring memories and nightmares of lost opportunities for reconciliation. Ellie's vendetta becomes an exhausting journey of pain, illustrated vividly in the confrontation with Nora, Abby's friend, where Ellie's actions mirror the violence inflicted on Joel.

Ellie's relentless pursuit of Abby, culminating in a violent clash, reflects her deep-seated trauma. Despite her opportunity to end Abby's life, visions of Joel — not as he died, but peacefully playing his guitar— prompt Ellie to halt her cycle of violence. This moment of clarity shows Ellie's realization that further vengeance will only erode what remains of her humanity. Joel's memory, in this light, becomes a saving grace, guiding her away from the brink.

Ellie's attempt to reclaim her life backfires as she returns to an empty home, and discovers that her injuries have made it impossible for her to connect with Joel's memory through music. The story of Ellie and Abby becomes a tale of mirrored losses and the futility of revenge, highlighting the heavy toll it takes on their souls. Both characters, having pushed their quests for vengeance to the brink, eventually recognize the emptiness it brings, with Abby losing her entire world in Seattle and Ellie losing Joel, Dina, and her cherished memories.

In the end, Ellie's departure from her empty home, leaving Joel's guitar behind, symbolizes a profound loss of self, a part of her that cannot be reclaimed. The narrative leaves both Ellie and Abby as reflections of each other — two individuals who traversed the depths of vengeance only to find that it led to a hollow victory, underscoring the game's meditation on the cost of revenge and the possibility of redemption, albeit at a great personal loss.

About the Author

ANGELO MIRRA studied psychology in Rome, at LUMSA University, where he graduated in clinical psychology. He then decided to continue his career in Rome to become a professional psychotherapist, joining a specialization school of psychoanalysis, where he is currently studying. Angelo is also very passionate about video games, having spent countless hours playing them since childhood. He once envisioned his life as a game designer, but at the end of high school, he chose psychology as a more realistic way to work and build a career. Nonetheless, Angelo has always kept his passion for gaming alive. In fact, he graduated with a thesis on video games and their impact on human behavior as a learning tool, never imagining that video games would reappear in his career path. After graduating, Angelo joined a PhD course in Learning Sciences and Digital Technologies, using his thesis as a project and continuing to study video games as an educational tool, particularly for social and relational skills and emotions. He is blending his PhD research with his psychoanalytic studies, taking an interest in video games from a psychoanalytic perspective as well. Angelo is currently working on a video game intended to serve as a therapeutic tool for hikikomori, aiming to connect with their internal world and help them become more aware of their emotions and heal their social ailments, offering a better way of life.

References

Freud, S. (1915). *Mourning and Melancholy.* In Freud Works Vol. 8. Bollati Boringhieri.

Freu, S. (1920). *Beyond the pleasure principle.* Bollati Boringhieri.

Klein, M., & Riviere, J., (1969). *Love, hate and reparation.* Astrolabio Publishing House.

Klein, M., & Jones, E. (2006). *Writings 1921-1958.* Bollati Boringhieri.

METAMORPHOSIS: PRESERVING LIFE'S MAGIC AGAINST THE BACKDROP OF TRAGEDY

TYLER W. SECOR

> *"I struggled for a long time with surviving. And, no matter what, you keep finding something to fight for."*
> —Joel, *The Last of Us: Part I*

Growing up is awkward and tragic, even under the best circumstances. Though Ellie and other kids face significant existential threats throughout the bleak tales of *The Last of Us*, the joys of life manage to break through. How does this happen? How is it that relationships bloom, communities flourish, and love thrives despite unspeakable hardship? Why and how do the characters choose to embrace life's magic rather than slink into darkness?

This chapter will explore how the kids, families, and communities within *The Last of Us* maintain resiliency in the face of trauma, abuse, significant loss, mass violence, and a pandemic. It will draw connections to our world's current climate, explore how relationships offer comfort and healing, and understand how the fullness of life can still be relished against seemingly insurmountable odds.

We begin with Joel Miller, who lives in a suburb of Austin, Texas, with his daughter, Sarah. He is a young, single father running a small business with his only sibling, Tommy, and struggling to make ends meet. After returning home late on his birthday, Sarah offers him a simple gift: a wristwatch. Little did they know this would be their last night together, and Joel would experience an earth-shattering moment he would carry for the rest of his life. In the early morning hours following Joel's birthday, Sarah wakes up to discover the initial moments of the cordyceps fungus pandemic outbreak. As she, Joel, and Tommy attempt to flee Austin by truck, and eventually by foot, Sarah is mortally wounded by a United States soldier. Joel held her in his arms, softly weeping as she died in agony.

In this moment, it became clear to players that *The Last of Us* was no ordinary video game. It would pull no punches, leave no dark stone unturned, nor show mercy to its characters. Despite this, *The Last of Us* is a critically acclaimed franchise that transcended its medium. The video games and TV series grossed millions globally, and moved countless people to embrace their explorations of life, love, and meaning. At its core, *The Last of Us* explores existentialism — a philosophy rooted in how human beings *choose* to live. Though it has many facets, one of existentialism's central concepts is that life is inherently meaningless. Another core theme is that we, and we alone, are responsible for our own lives and happiness.

But what is happiness, anyway? Positive psychology tells us it is essentially our sense of "subjective well-being," and combines three aspects: evaluative, eudemonic, and affective. Broadly defined, these terms mean:

- Evaluative: How fulfilled or satisfied one feels with their life.
- Eudemonic: What a person's sense of meaning and purpose are.

- Affective: How much positive and negative emotion a person tends to feel when zooming out and looking at the big picture.

According to positive psychology, happiness involves much more than feeling positive emotions such as joy, contentment, satisfaction, or excitement. Positive feelings play an important role, but happiness is not a state of being — it is a *way* of being. Happiness is not just a choice, but a series of choices a person makes every day. This is not to suggest that the trauma, loss, or any other terrible things the characters (or those of us in the real world) experience can simply be sent away at will. Rather, when combining positive psychology and existentialism, *The Last of Us* challenges players to *choose* to live full and meaningful lives.

Consider Joel's unimaginable tragedy. Players do not need to be parents themselves to share in Joel's anguish or be profoundly impacted by those opening minutes. While this was only the beginning of Joel's trauma, by the end he chooses to live his life fully and without regret. He rediscovers himself, finds love and joy, and creates meaning in the wake of any parent's worst nightmare. When all was said and done, Joel chose to be happy. What led to such a striking paradigm shift?

 I'VE BEEN ON BOTH SIDES

Following Sarah's death, Joel awakens 20 years later in the Boston Quarantine Zone, working with a woman named Tess to smuggle contraband in and out of the city. Joel has clearly grown hardened over the 20-year gap, as we witness cryptic comments about moral ambiguity, see him somberly burning bodies of the dead (including children), and acting violently toward other non-playable characters (NPCs) in the story's first act. Joel and

Tess are tasked with smuggling 14-year-old Ellie Williams (or "cargo," as Joel initially refers to her) out of the city. Joel and Tess quickly discover that Ellie is infected, though appears immune to the infection. During their journey out of the city, Tess also becomes infected, and after seeing that her infection quickly worsened while Ellie's did not develop, spends her final moments pleading with Joel to escort Ellie across the country. For Joel, Tess has been the only semblance of human connection he maintained since his daughter's death, so he begrudgingly accepts her plea.

Despite Joel's efforts to remain emotionally disconnected from Ellie, she wears him down throughout their journey. She does things that Joel finds funny or endearing, like reading to him from a cringey dad-joke book, collecting comics, and sneaking toys in their cargo. She inspires a protectiveness in him by insisting on having a gun, even though Joel believes she is not ready for the responsibility. Most importantly, Ellie breaks down his emotional walls by asking him all sorts of personal questions (while brazenly scoffing past his dismissive non-responses), and pushes Joel into conversations and relationships he would otherwise have avoided. Ellie challenged Joel to reconsider how he has been merely surviving instead of fully living.

Joel has experienced many significant losses during and before the events of *The Last of Us*, most of which the player has not witnessed. When a person experiences a significant loss, grief follows. Grief is a psychological and (often heavily) emotional process in which a person makes sense of a significant loss. Joel's most significant losses that the player observes are the deaths of Sarah and Tess. However, it is critical to recognize that while significant losses often include death, death is not required for a person to experience grief. Little is known about Joel's life during the 20 years following Sarah's death, though he makes it clear he committed heinous and terrible acts to survive. This is evident when, after surviving a violent ambush where the attackers pretend to be wounded, Ellie asks how Joel knew the person was lying. Joel soberly answered, "I've been on both sides." In this scenario, Joel reflects that he sacrifices pieces of himself to survive. He needs to shut off parts of his heart and mind to withstand the emotional burden of the violent acts he does to keep himself and his community alive. Joel is a fragmented man, evidenced by his ability to compartmentalize (or section and close off) parts of who he is. Ellie does not yet understand this, and pushes Joel throughout their journey to openly discuss the parts of himself he so carefully closes away.

For example, Joel and Ellie find themselves allied with two brothers, a young adult and a teenager named Henry and Sam Burrell. Together the group manages to escape a dangerous situation being hunted by a larger group of people. After the struggle, the younger brother, Sam, becomes infected and was shot and killed by the older brother, Henry. Distraught, hopeless, and faced with circumstances parallel to Joel and Sarah, Henry turns the gun on himself and dies by suicide as Joel and Ellie look on.

Not long after, Ellie attempts to process her grief through talking about it with Joel. Ellie experiences disenfranchised grief — grief that is unacknowledged — in every attempt she makes to have conversations with Joel about the deaths they witnessed. Joel tells her shortly after Tess's death that he will not discuss Tess with Ellie. When Ellie discovers a grave with a small teddy bear, she mentions Sam, and Joel shuts her down. Ellie said, What? I want to talk about it." Joel ultimately responded, "No. Things happen, and we move on." By this juncture, players can easily see how compartmentalized Joel is, and how he has lost parts of himself to endure following his traumatic experiences.

 I WANT TO TALK ABOUT IT

Summer turns to fall as they reconnect with Joel's brother, Tommy, in Wyoming. Joel feels his heart opening to Ellie, notices himself becoming protective of her, and panics. For Joel, Henry and Sam are a sobering and terrifying reminder of what is at stake if he opens his heart up to Ellie. Although Joel tries to hide his hesitation from Ellie, she feels Joel distancing himself from her. This does not slow Ellie down, as she continues to try connecting with him.

Joel feels conflicted about caring for Ellie. He begins to see her in as a daughter and feels powerless when cannot always protect her. He draws clear parallels between Ellie and Sarah, and fears another failure if he is unable to protect Ellie from harm. Unable to reconcile his feelings, Joel tries to convince Tommy to take Ellie and complete their journey on Joel's behalf. Ellie quickly discovers this, sees it as a betrayal, and runs away. Joel and Tommy run after her and find her in a bedroom of an abandoned house reading an old teenage girl's diary.

Ellie muses about how kids before the pandemic were carefree, adding that she never enjoyed a privileged life without constant traumatic and existential threats. Joel dismisses Ellie's musings, scolds her for running away, and demands she accompany him back to Tommy's community. Ellie stands her ground and confronts Joel about his fear of losing her — and declared to him that she is not Sarah. This strikes a nerve in Joel, and he warns Ellie to tread lightly. His response demonstrates his conflicted feelings about Ellie, who he is someone he clearly loves but finds challenging. Regardless of Joel's best efforts, compartmentalizing his feelings would not serve him in this exchange. He does not attempt to scream, threaten, or intimidate Ellie. Rather, he acknowledges his pain about Sarah and warns Ellie to be careful with her next words. By doing this, Joel creates room for a conversation and provides Ellie the opportunity to respectfully speak her mind. Ellie pleads with Joel, sharing that she had lost everyone she ever cared for, that Joel is the only family she is ever known, and that she is scared. While Ellie had broken through more than anyone had, Joel is still not ready to fully accept Ellie into his heart. He coldly tells her that she is not his daughter, he is not her father, and that they would part ways.

Ellie, Joel, and Tommy take a quiet and tense ride back to the community. Joel is seen behind Ellie — looking at her with pain, longing, and regret. Joel now starts to consciously realize and accept how deeply he cares for Ellie. When they arrive at the community, Joel declares that he and Ellie were leaving immediately to complete their journey together. Tommy insists they at least stay the night, but Joel's mind was made up. Finally, he embraces new meaning and purpose in adopting Ellie.

 WASN'T TIME THAT DID IT

Fall turns to winter and Joel is severely wounded while fleeing scavengers, tasking Ellie with his care and their survival. Ellie demonstrates her quick wit and resourcefulness by finding shelter, keeping Joel alive, and hunting for food. On a hunt she encounters David, a seemingly friendly middle-aged man who offers Ellie safety in his community. Ellie feels uneasy with David and declines his invitation, but negotiates with him for antibiotics. As Ellie and David await the medicine, they encounter a swath of infected, forcing an alliance between her and David to fight off the infected. As Ellie slowly lowers her guard with David, he reveals that he sent the group of scavengers that she encountered with Joel, and that David intends to take Ellie in and kill Joel in retribution for his lost men. David captures Ellie, and she realizes that David lives in a cannibalistic community and abuses young girls and women. He intends for Ellie to choose her own fate — submit to David, or be eaten. Ellie refuses, and escapes by biting David's finger and killing David's companion. David tracks her down and corners her. David overpowers Ellie and tells her she has no idea what he is "capable of." In the struggle, Ellie grabs hold of David's machete and turns it on him. Joel finds her as she is still heaving the machete and pulls her off David.

This experience is not only a critical moment in Joel and Ellie's relationship; it is also a flashpoint in Ellie's personal journey. Ellie's assumptive world shatters as she realizes not only Joel's vulnerability, but her own. Part of grieving, especially after experiencing a significant loss for the first time, is this concept of the "assumptive world." Everyone has an assumptive world, which is the way that we experience, interpret, and make sense of the world around us. Our assumptive world is where we get ideas about how the world works, of ourselves, families, people, culture, and relationships, of right and wrong, and how our lives have gone and have yet to go. After a significant loss, that assumptive world is shattered, and it suddenly becomes clear to people just how vulnerable they and their lives are.

Ellie's assumptions and views of herself, the world, and perceived safety were challenged by David and his community. They physically wounded Joel, and spiritually and emotionally wounded Ellie. She sees darkness like she has never experienced, yet still finds the strength to survive. She learned what she is capable of doing to survive and protect her loved ones. It also created a richer awareness of Joel's hesitation to love her, and drew uncomfortable parallels between David's actions and her own. While many of David's actions were heinous, evil, and unacceptable, some (such as the cannibalism) were committed to preserve and protect his community. David was not purely good or evil, he was just a person who did both good and evil things. This experience planted the seed that would drive Ellie's inner conflict in *The Last of Us: Part II*.

Winter turns to spring as Joel and Ellie reach their final destination of Salt Lake City. In contrast to their established dynamic, Joel is chatty while Ellie remains somber and dissociated. It is unclear what is on Ellie's mind in that moment, but she is disengaged with Joel. She is in the early stages of reconciling life's inherent meaninglessness, just as Joel exits that same journey. Joel has spent decades grappling with Sarah's unnecessary death not at the hands of the infected, but of other people. By his own report, he has committed untold heinous acts living a life dedicated to survival. Survival is his purpose, and being alive is his only meaning. Yet when he meets Ellie, she awakes something in Joel he thought was long dead. She confronts him with his resilient capacity for love. Ellie *becomes* his purpose, and protecting and raising her become his meaning.

As they navigate the abandoned Salt Lake City streets, Joel finally answers one of Ellie's questions, and reveals that his hearing loss and the scar on his head are from a failed suicide attempt. Joel discloses that, through Sarah's death, he felt he had no purpose, adding that he has since been able to *create* new meaning. Ellie commented, "So time heals all wounds, I guess." Joel responded, "It wasn't time that did it." Ellie's eyes widen as she begins to understand that Joel had found new purpose in her, and found new meaning in his life. Joel made a conscious decision to love Ellie despite the risk. In the hazy dissociative fog, she navigates, she now sees Joel as a source of light and comfort. Joel does not try to take away or diminish her pain. Rather, he becomes a fellow traveler, and walked alongside her in the fog. This moment would be their closest.

 IT CAN'T BE FOR NOTHING

The duo continues their journey to St. Mary's Hospital in Salt Lake City. Joel shares stories of his life with Sarah, and Ellie hands him a picture of Joel and Sarah that she had stolen from Tommy back in Wyoming. Joel chokes up and finally acknowledges that, "no matter how hard you try, you can't escape your past." Shortly after they encountered giraffes from the ruins of the Salt Lake Zoo, Ellie allows herself to feel excited and embrace the magic of seeing giraffes. Joel notices this, and tells her they do not have to go through with this; that Ellie could choose to walk away and live a full life. Ellie ponders for a moment, considering their journey and all it entailed up to that point, and replies, "After everything we've been through ... everything I've done ... it can't be for nothing." Joel understands that Ellie needs to find meaning in her suffering, and that she thinks the only to do that was to harness her cure and save humanity. While Joel disagrees, the respects her wishes through silence and delivers her to the Fireflies.

When they reach their destination, Joel learns that creating a cure would require Ellie's death. As he considers his past failures, his moral ambiguity and shortcomings, and the decades he spent in violence and meaninglessness — what matters most is his love for Ellie., He decides that nothing is worth her life, and tells the Fireflies he will not accept Ellie's death. When they refuse to release Ellie, Joel kills dozens of them, including the doctor who was about to perform the surgery on Ellie. Ellie knows none of this, and wakes as she and Joel were driving out of the city. Joel lies to Ellie, claiming that the Fireflies no longer needed Ellie to perform the surgery because a cure was not possible.

Ellie later confronts Joel about his lie, expressing guilt for surviving when everyone else she knows and loves did not. Ellie experiences survivor's guilt — a profound sadness and guilt for living when many others did not. Joel acknowledges her survivor's guilt, rubbing the wristwatch Sarah gave him all those years ago, and sharing that he "struggled for a long time with surviving [Sarah], and no matter what…you keep finding something to fight for." In sharing his experience, Joel tells Ellie that her life can still be meaningful, and that she can find or create new purpose. Joel to Ellie that he is telling the truth about what happened at the hospital. Ellie outwardly accepts his response, but suspects he is lying to her. Though Joel believes he is acting in Ellie's best interest, his lie creates a rift between them that would outlast him.

 IF I EVER WERE TO LOSE YOU,  I'D SURELY LOSE MYSELF

As time goes on, Ellie and Joel built community in the remote Wyoming town of Jackson. Joel now has a girlfriend, and Ellie has also started dating, as well as making new friends — Dina and Jesse. Joel honors his promise of teaching Ellie to play guitar, and explores hobbies of his own. Despite the growing rift between them, those years in Jackson were some of the best and happiest in their lives. This was the happiness Joel chose — a life with Ellie in which he found joy in small moments. It was the happiest and safest either of them felt within memory —until it was so longer.

On an early March afternoon, Joel, Tommy, Ellie, Dina, and Jesse split into groups to patrol the area surrounding Jackson when a blizzard struck. Joel and Tommy encountered a young woman named Abby Anderson alone in the blizzard. Abby was being swarmed by the infected, and Tommy and Joel rescue her. To escape the danger, Abby leads them back to her camp, where her friends were lying in wait. Because Joel now lives peacefully, he is no longer tense and on guard in the same way he was before meeting Ellie.

While Joel's guard is down, Abby attacks him and instructs Joel to guess her identity. Joel replies, "Why don't you say whatever speech you got rehearsed and get this over with." Joel accepts his fate, and does not resist, fight back, or plead for his life. He is old and tired, at peace with his choices, and satisfied with his life. From Joel's position, he had pressed on after unspeakable hardship, and found joy, purpose, and fulfillment in his relationship raising Ellie. Not because of the cruel and unforgiving world that they lived in, but in spite of it. Ellie discovers Joel's whereabouts just before his final moments, and Abby's friends restrain Ellie so she cannot intervene. While ignoring Ellie's pleading, Abby ends Joel's life in front of her.

This moment sends Ellie into a vengeful tailspin. Vowing justice, she, Tommy, Dina, and Jesse make their way to Seattle searching for Abby and her friends. Ellie's is overcome with grief, as she reflects on memories with Joel. Ellie's grief is complicated by the trauma of Joel's lie, the circumstances of his death, and her lingering guilt about the distance she put between them. Ellie cannot separate her desire for revenge with her grief, and loses herself in the process.

 I WANT WHAT YOU WANT

It becomes clear that Abby and her crew had come to Jackson specifically searching for Joel. Abby is a Firefly whose father was Jerry Anderson, the surgeon that Joel murdered in Salt Lake City to rescue Ellie. Further, Abby's crew were also Fireflies posted at Salt Lake City, and greatly impacted by Joel's decision to kill members of their community. Abby spent five years training and searching for Joel to exact revenge. For Abby, her purpose rests in avenging her father and killing Joel. Yet, as we see throughout the events of *The Last of Us: Part II*, Abby does not find resolution from murdering Joel. Instead, she feels guiltier and it creates a rift with her friends.

The person closest to Abby is her friend and former lover, Owen Moore. Owen was also a Firefly stationed in Salt Lake City with Abby, and their then-romantic relationship grew complex after Abby's father was killed. The only time the player sees Abby, Owen, and Jerry together was in Abby's memory of her Jerry at the zoo in Salt Lake City on the same day he was killed. It is clear in this sequence that Jerry and Abby had a close and loving relationship. Later, when Abby discovers her father's body, Owen is the one who holds and comforts her as she cries.

Owen always supported Abby in her mission to avenge her father, often telling her, "I want what you want." However, Owen loved Abby deeply, and made many attempts to connect with her and help her find joy. Owen also grieved for Jerry, yet manages to explore interests and develop hobbies, tries to foster a relationship with Abby, and breaks rules and has fun. At times, he is able to engage Abby in his pursuits, such as sneaking off from training to show her the aquarium, goading Abby into a shooting competition, or having her try his homemade liquor.

HEY, YOU'RE MY PEOPLE

Owen and Abby broke up because Abby was unable to relinquish her single-minded goal of killing Joel. When Owen confronted Abby about this, he shares the guilt he feels over killing Joel and many others, adding that he does not want to live his life that way anymore. Owen recognizes that he will not find meaning or purpose in othering or killing people. Rather, he finds meaning and purpose in the small things, such as his relationship with Abby, playing games, exploring his hobbies, and working on projects.

Over time, Abby feels the gap widening between her and Owen, yet their relationship never fully dwindled. When Owen goes missing from the WLF, Abby sneaks away against orders to find him. On her way, she encounters two kids from an enemy faction known as the Seraphites. The Seraphites are a religious group warring with the WLF over territory. The Seraphite kids were siblings, Yara and Lev, who fled the group after Lev came out as transgender and shaved his head to look like one of the men. Abby rescues them from danger and leaves them alone to find Owen. After discovering Owen at the aquarium, Abby has a nightmare of walking into the room where she found her father's body to instead see Yara and Lev dead. Abby sees this nightmare as a call to support Yara and Lev, and goes to great lengths rescuing them and bringing them back to the aquarium.

The following night, Abby dreams of opening the same door to discover her father, who turns around and smiles proudly. She found no peace from killing Joel, and it causes her friend group to splinter and grow further apart. Yet, in spending time with Owen, and helping Yara and Lev, Abby starts to feel satisfaction and purpose. She creates meaning through service and community, and starts to picture a full and nuanced life for herself.

 WE CAN CHOOSE TO BE HAPPY

Each character in *The Last of Us* is confronted with significant loss, violence, and trauma. Yet, many find and create meaning following tragedy. Joel, after losing his daughter and committing heinous acts, found meaning and love through protecting and raising Ellie. Ellie found it through her relationships, hobbies, and interests. Bill and Frank made it through sharing meals, rebuilding their town, working through disagreements, eating strawberries, and sharing friendships. Abby created it through self-forgiveness and embracing relationships and community. Lev discovered it through living authentically in all facets of his life.

In one of their last conversations, Owen pleads with Abby to leave Seattle to search for the Fireflies with him. Before Abby can protest, Owen says, "I know it's a fucking mess, but we can choose to be happy." Owen understood early on what many of the characters spend their lives searching for: that happiness is not only positive feelings. More importantly, happiness is a choice.

Positive psychology tells us happiness includes positive feelings (like contentment, satisfaction, and joy), and a person's sense of meaning and purpose in their lives. Owen understands that, while we cannot always control our circumstances or how we feel, we can *choose* how to respond to our feelings and circumstances. Even in the face of unspeakable pain, we can *choose* to find and create meaning. We can *choose* to cherish relationships, embrace interests and hobbies, explore our surroundings, and carry ourselves with authenticity.

The characters in *The Last of Us* explore how different people and communities experience and respond to existentialism, significant loss and grief, mass and personal violence, and crises of identity. And yet, with each devastating blow come equally uplifting payoffs. Players also witness how love can create joy and meaning, even against the worst circumstances. The franchise shows many examples of people of all ages and backgrounds choosing to embrace life in its fullness. Ultimately, *The Last of Us* can be interpreted as a call to action that confronts players with our own power: the power to choose.

About the Author

TYLER W. SECOR, MS, LPC is a clinical mental health counselor practicing in Wisconsin. He predominantly practices from psychodynamic, person-centered, existential, and feminist perspectives. Tyler works with clients of all ages at A New Breath(e) of Life Counseling and Consulting, an outpatient mental health clinic in Brookfield, WI. He is currently a doctoral student for Counselor Education and Supervision at Mount Mary University in Milwaukee, WI. Tyler has been a die hard fan of *The Last of Us* since the *Part I*'s release in 2013, and is eager to bridge the franchise with his passions for therapy, psychology, and existentialism. He is also passionate about lifting negative stigma surrounding video gamers and games, and recognizes the therapeutic potential of video gaming.

References

Doka, K. (1989). Disenfranchised grief. In K. Doka (Ed.), Disenfranchised grief: Recognizing hidden sorrow (pp. 13-23). Lexington, MA: Lexington Books.

Parkes, C. M. (1975). Determinants of outcome following bereavement. Omega, 6,303-323

Seligman, M. E., & Csikszentmihalyi, M. (2000). *Positive psychology: An introduction* (Vol. 55, No. 1, p. 5). American Psychological Association.

Van der Kolk, B. A. (2015). *The body keeps the score : brain, mind, and body in the healing of trauma.* Penguin Books.

Yalom, I. D. (1980). *Existential psychotherapy.* Basic Books.

FINDING THE 'WHY': RESILIENCE THROUGH THE EYES OF *THE LAST OF US*

MELINDA KORTE

> "He who has a 'why' to live for can bear almost any 'how'."
> —Friedrich Nietzsche

The postapocalyptic world of Naughty Dog's 2013 classic video game *The Last of Us* is a landscape painted by death, decay, and traumatic responses. For the last ten years, this game has gripped the attention of international audiences through a variety of media, including multiple video games, graphic novels, theater productions, and — most recently— television. There are countless ways to observe the impact of *The Last of Us* on popular culture, particularly in a worldscape shaped by the aftermath of the COVID-19 pandemic. One could argue it is no accident that post-apocalyptic games— a popular genre even before the pandemic— spiked in consumption after lockdown started. But why do stories, such as the narratives of *The Last of Us*, draw people in? Why would audiences voluntarily choose to consume content that consistently triggers intense emotions through devastation, loss, and trauma?

It may seem obvious to just generally consider that they are great games ... but we can also consider *why* these games are so great. In the tumultuous divided world of 2024, it is important we understand *why* humans are drawn to certain types of media. Ultimately, the simplest answer is that our external lives reflects our internal ones. Things like our hobbies, relationships, communication styles, maladaptive habits, and career patterns shed light on the state of an individual's internal world, such as their body, brain, and psyche. Understanding the qualities of one's internal landscape enables the individual to take proactive selfcare, find meaning in life, and prevent stressors to the best of their capability. Whether that individual is coming to terms with the reality of death, exploring the bleak outlook they feel stuck in, recognizing their capacity for brutality, evaluating identity formation, or coming to terms with trauma, *The Last of Us* holds a safe space for players to identify with the darkness they see within themselves — acted out through the lives of these characters.

INNER DARKNESS AND PSYCHOLOGICAL PROJECTION

Anthony Bean outlines the various ways that gamers psychologically project onto the games they play as an unconscious means of immersing in a reality they can relate to. Because *The Last of Us* is now accessible across multiple types of media, this concept remains true regardless of how it is consumed (cinema, gaming, reading, cosplay, etc.). He also elaborates that therapists and researchers alike are starting to realize that audience engagement with content from *The Last of Us* holds "immense potential to work with many clinical disorders and to help many heal through posttraumatic growth." Whether people can connect with the characters themselves, or to the myriad of therapeutic themes that emerge from their lives (sexual abuse/assault, grief/loss, abandonment, neglect, starvation, foster care, mental illness, etc.), the concept is the same — audiences immerse themselves in *The Last of Us* universe to find cathartic relief.

Though there are many captivating elements within *The Last of Us* universe, one of its most impactful themes is the visceral presentation of resilience and posttraumatic growth. This universe has some of the most psychologically complicated storytelling in modern video gaming, along with a multifaceted storyline. The depth of these characters intersects with the terror of their world to demonstrate the intense, multilayered nuances of trauma, posttraumatic growth, and adversity's destructive impact on human development. The high-quality storytelling experiences in this universe show that it is possible to move through trauma using one's psychological Swiss army knife: resilience. But most of all, these stories portray the diverse complexities of love as well as the strength of connections built in adversity — such as the relationship between Ellie and Joel. In essence, the humanistic vulnerability of these stories demonstrates the resilience of the human spirit while simultaneously communicating to the audience, *You are not alone.*

These characters demonstrate that to survive requires adapting to the environment and allowing a sense of purpose and meaning to reflect the needs of each moment. Characters who lose their will to live are usually those that no longer perceive meaning in their suffering; for example, in *Part I*,,Henry's split-second response after realizing that his brother, Sam, was dead. Those who survive are driven by a sense of purpose, whether that is a farm in the country with their loving family, or a fixation on revenge.

The inspiring characters in *The Last of Us* universe consistently exhibit the power of human potential by questioning how far their limits can stretch when presented with traumatic stress. Perhaps viewers are also fascinated by the reality that two people could experience a similar trauma, and yet live very different journeys (such as with Ellie and Abby). Maybe the journeys of these characters captivate our curiosities as a mirror for how we might handle the same scenarios? Regardless, *The Last of Us* features a heart-wrenching spectrum of experiences with characters that exist across a range from hopeful to despondent.

INTERNATIONAL INFLUENCE MEETS INTRAPERSONAL IMPACT

The notions of 'good' and 'evil' exist as controversial constructs throughout *Parts I* and *II* of *The Last of Us*, challenging human cognitive flexibility and perception of humanity. There is much to learn from the intensity of these characters, the lives they lead, the choices they make, and their responses to the world around them — for better or worse. Whether audiences are moved by character interactions with cannibal camp leader David in *Part I*, or the Washington Liberation Front (WLFs) in *Part II*, they are still learning something about themselves.

Projecting onto this type of media allows the player to think about the choices, emotions, thoughts, and morals they may embody in the same situation. Additionally, audiences may even compare game events to the adversity they experience within their everyday reality. They may find themselves identifying and the 'good guys' from the 'bad guys.' However, perhaps what is actually most important for audiences here are answers to the questions, *Where do I fit in here? Am I good or evil?* In reality, good and evil are constructs unique to human perspective, interaction, culture, and time. But perhaps consumers use these games in part to measure their own sense of humanity?

Google statistics featured in Figure 1[1] are clearly indicate the wide reach of *The Last of Us* . In June 2013, the international number of Google searches for the real-life zombie-ant fungus, known as cordyceps, saw a moderate spike — thus indicating some viewer interest

---

[1] Graph of trends for Google searches related to cordyceps since December 1st, 2010.

in the science behind the horrors of the infected. This correlates with the release of the original game-(*Part I*) in 2013. However, Figure 1 also demonstrates the dramatic increase of these statistics following the premier of HBO's acclaimed television series in 2022. The right side of this graph demonstrates that the spike in searches continued into 2024. Essentially, "cordyceps" is now one of the highest trending search terms on Google internationally.

However, this fear of cordyceps comes at a time when the world is more stable than I was in March 2020. We now know more about COVID-19 and are farther removed from the unsettling pandemic that took the world by storm in many ways. *The Last of Us* and its science-fiction portrayal of the cordyceps-fueled apocalypse provides a new platform for international empathy. On some level, the audience recognizes that this arguably *could* have been us... but thankfully was not. Therefore, this reality allows us to enjoy *The Last of Us* — immerse in it, cry together, and move through the lives of these characters with just enough space that we can empathize while recognizing that this world is not our own. It is *just* real enough.

Figure 1

Giulia Hayward from NPR wrote of the cordyceps that:

"Ophiocordyceps unilateralis, otherwise known as cordyceps or zombie-ant fungus, infects insects such as ants or spiders. Like other parasites, cordyceps drains its host completely of nutrients before filling its body with spores that will let the fungus reproduce. It then compels the insect to seek height and remain there before it expels these spores, infecting other nearby insects in the process."

What is it about cordyceps that captivates the audience's curiosity? Is it the all-too-real way that the apocalypse could be instigated by a small, rare fungus primarily found in the mountains of Southeast Asia that has been historically used medicinally for three hundred years? Is it the gruesome transformations that the infected endure in their various forms?

Possible fears and motivations are infinite. Regardless of the individual reason, this data clearly illustrates that cordyceps and *The Last of Us* struck a chord with many players.

MORALITY ADAPTS TO TRAUMATIC CONTAGIONS

At the onset of the cordyceps outbreak, the characters of this universe are thrown overnight into a world that is a shadow of its past, and into lives that demand entirely new meaning to survive. While all characters in *The Last of Us* experience unique journeys, they share a common trauma: losing their loved ones unexpectedly in often-gruesome fashions. Some characters are forced to watch these deaths unfold in real-time. Others are tasked with personally taking their loved one's life as final gestures of love and mercy.

Overall, the dangers of this new world require an adjustment of the character's morals, values, and identity to survive. They are forced to make high-stakes choices that constantly challenge their sense of right and wrong, good and evil. While these choices sometimes provide new opportunities for renewed meaning or positivity (such as Joel bonding with Ellie and getting a chance to heal old wounds), they often come with significant consequences and responsibility. People who would have otherwise been non-violent or person-centered now may make decisions that would have previously violated their moral code in the world before the outbreak.

For example, before he was killed by Joel in the Salt Lake City Firefly Lab, Dr. Jerry Anderson was prepared to sacrifice Ellie without her consent in hope of creating a vaccine for the cordyceps infection. In fact, he is confronted by Maureen— the leader of the Fireflies — for his callous reference to Ellie as" the host," dehumanizing her as he prepares to" separate the specimen" from her brain. During this argument, Maureen reminds him, "She's a child ... what if this was Abby?"

In response, Dr. Anderson does not waiver in his motivation. He brushes the question aside, because he can— the reality is that his daughter is safe, and a stranger holds the potential to cure the world. He revisits his ethical training as a surgeon— a moral code that he held prior to the fall —and takes a new approach to align with the needs of the new world order. This is just one of many examples showcased throughout the universe's content.

MAN'S NEW SEARCH FOR MEANING

Upon reflection, these narratives are similar to those of the pioneering 20th -century psychiatrist, Viktor Frankl; the resilient survivor of four Holocaust concentration camps, including Auschwitz. His book, *Man's Search for Meaning*, is still referenced as a template for treating psychological suffering since being first published in 1946. In this text, Frankl processed his years as a prisoner of war and detailed his traumatic brushes with death to elaborate on his foundational logotherapy concept;i.e. finding motivation in what Frankl calls "will to meaning". Pervasive throughout *The Last of Us,* will to meaning is the existential notion that living requires suffering, while survival requires one to find meaning. As a result, one's perceived meaning in life becomes the motivator for action.

Frankl centered his entire psychotherapeutic approach around this Nietzsche-inspired philosophical ideal and believed that without a will to meaning, one would lose the desire to live. Frankl researched the influence of will to meaning in connection with the decline of physical and mental wellbeing throughout his professional life. For example, he studied how one's perceived meaning influenced their individual purpose in life. If one did not perceive substantial purpose and meaning, then this would be reflected in their quality of life and will to live. Not only is this true for aging adults, it is also applicable for those struggling with anxiety, depression, or other mental illnesses. It is especially applicable for those that struggle with suicidal behavior and ideation. Fundamentally, Frankl believed that interruptions to wellness or quality of life had existential roots connected to our will to meaning. Some of his most poignant research was based on firsthand experience during his time imprisoned in concentration camps.

His work has continued to inspire generations of people around the world, and has been translated into 21 other languages over the last 60 years. Frankl's teachings remain particularly relevant during the aftermath of the 2020 pandemic. In a time that made *The Last of Us* feel all too real, the world shared common trauma and prolonged isolation. Throughout quarantine, people's lives were impacted by so many unknown variables apart from several constants: loss, fear, and death.

Only a few months after lockdown began in 2020, the long-anticipated sequel to *The Last of Us* was released, quickly becoming an international phenomenon. It can be speculated that the game's success was its partly due to this fictionalized, an existential escape, which enabled the consumer to connect with shared experiences and fears. The world within *The Last of Us Part I* and *II* is one of instability, survival, constant battles between life and death, anxiety, and fear. Though that world is different from the one we live in, those feelings felt all too similar during the COVID-19 lockdown. It is for this reason that – regardless of media consumed by the viewer (comic, short story, fan art, video game, etc.) — *The Last of Us* continues to provide a means to process traumatic stress, relate with others' inner darkness, and experience validation by popular culture.

TRAUMA AND RESILIENCE

Within their crisis and trauma textbook used for counselor training, Owens and Parsons pair the word "resilience" with others like "energy despite exhaustion…. hardiness… [and] optimism," and remind their readers that resilience is either a preexisting or acquired trait in those who experience posttraumatic growth. Important pioneers in the world of psychotherapy, such as Yalom, Frankl, and Miller, use positive psychology and existential philosophy as cornerstones for their healing methods, which ultimately strive for the development of resilience in their clients. The American Psychiatric Association identifies one's ability to be resilient as one of many key indicators for various mental illnesses in the Diagnostic and Statistical Manual of Mental Disorders, Text Revision (DSM-5-TR). This reality suggests that resilience is a trait which humans should strive for. In fact, it seems to be a core gauge of mind-body wellness.

This is why resilience is so important in the context of *The Last of Us* universe; the characters who live resiliently, and in ways that align with their will to meaning, are the happiest characters. Even during a global outbreak, they manage to find fulfillment. A great example of a character with this trait is Dina. After the events of *Part II*, she would be perfectly content living out her life with Ellie and JJ at the farmhouse outside Jackson Hole. She and Ellie both experienced trauma in Seattle, yet she seems to be adjusted enough to experience joy, feel loved by her family, and carry out day-to-day tasks as needed. She can function and thrive in some ways, despite the trauma she has experienced, and is not plagued by a need for revenge, like Ellie. This is not to say that Ellie does not also demonstrate resilience; but to say that Dina is the strongest example of a character who embodies will to meaning as a catalyst for posttraumatic growth.

Aside from the game's emotional immersion, audiences are awed by the endurance of each character's unique journey through traumatic stress, regardless of the outcome. In *Part II*, viewers are confronted with Ellie's counterpart and the dual protagonist, Abby, as well as the difficult emotions that her controversial actions arouse. But controversies aside, it is undeniable that the same resilience and inner strength within Ellie and Joel lives within Abby. Despite the differences in their origins, they share similar actions, thoughts, traumas, and stories.. Both these games are a testament to visceral intensity of trauma and the resilience that comes from growing through it. Audiences get to watch as trauma changes each character over time, their innocence melts away, and their personalities evolve in response to their need for strength.

Ellie — who was once a high-energy, optimistic, pun-loving child — becomes self-reproachful, reclusive, and distrustful. In *Part I*, she is quick to connect with people she meets along the way. But in *Part II*, she has difficulty even relying on her friends and loved ones. Survivor's guilt and the choice that Joel made at the end of *Part I* seems to heavily influence this shift in her personality.

Joel's character development goes full circle from a loving and doting father to a cold, survival-oriented smuggler, to a man who will do whatever it takes to keep his loved ones safe, no matter the cost. The television depiction of his character highlights his emotional complexities and reasons behind making the difficult, often evocative, choices that he does. But at the end of the day, Joel feels love so strongly that he would kill a whole hospital of strangers, including the only surgeon who may be able to make a vaccine to save humanity, if that means that his loved one may live— even if it also means she m never speak to him again.

Abby, once filled with future-oriented dreams and optimism, uses her time with the WLF to focus on physical strength to cope with the loss of her father. She directs her revenge and desire to kill Joel into every Scar faction member she kills. In fact, she is quite good at it and is heralded as one of Isaac's top soldiers. However, *Part II* challenges Abby's sense of good and evil (e.g. who deserves to live and die) when she meets the Seraphite siblings, Lev and Yara. It is through this initially tense relationship that she is reminded of the other parts of living that make us whole; faith, belonging, and connection.

While it is a model of strength and post-traumatic growth, *The Last of Us* franchise also gives players a place to process their meaning in life as well as their temperamental existence. If Ellie and Joel can countlessly sidestep death at the hand of humans and infected alike, then the player may feel inspired to harness will to meaning in fighting their own dilemmas. As the pair is exposed to severe abuse, physical duress, and dangerous groupthink, the player can escape, externalize, process, and hold space for their own emotional *infection*.

 INFECTED WILL TO MEANING

Fans of *The Last of Us* universe were relieved to find out that cordyceps cannot survive at the internal temperature of human bodies, thus making this version of the apocalypse highly unlikely without divine intervention and/or fungal evolutionary prowess. Nonetheless, this terrifying example of science fiction seems to hold a firm grip on the curiosities of its audiences, and people are captivated by the characters in this timeline.

But when one takes a closer look beyond the science and between the lines of the storytelling, there lies an interesting metaphor for other infections that can impact humans. In fact, there is one infectious entity that devastates the quality of human health in all domains of functioning in both short and long-term doses: hopelessness.

This psycho-emotional infection of sorts eats away our desire to live and ability to perceive a future. It begins to control bodily experiences and impairs independent functioning, manifesting as issues like chronic pain, inflammation of cells (putting one at higher risk for cancer), weakening the immune system, neurodegeneration, and unhealthy lifestyle patterns that can be fatal over time. Mentally, it manipulates our thoughts and can create life altering cognitive distortions which may take over our personality, identity, core values, and outlook on living. Hopelessness is a metaphoric infection, internationally researched as one of the loudest warning signs of suicide.

Many healthcare fields (psychiatry, psychology, counseling, allied clinical therapies) acknowledge hopelessness as an emotional experience that can hold one emotionally hostage in mental illness, addiction, grief, and despair. Even from outside of the world of therapy, medical professionals are now recognizing the impact of hopelessness of patient responsivity and outcomes to treatment. The Turkish Journal of Psychiatric Nursing published a systematic review on this topic, sharing results from 18 qualitative and quantitative studies published between 2016 and 2022 in several countries: USA, Canada, United Kingdom, and China. In total, these 18 studies collected data from 43,737 individuals aged between 18 and 30. As a result of this comprehensive project, the researchers substantiated that, "Hopelessness was an important predictor.... A risk factor for suicidal ideation and suicidal behavior." Moreover, long-term follow-up data in these studies demonstrated that hopelessness was heavily connected to suicide attempts and completions by participants. The researchers explained that "perception of being a burden," lack of perceived belonging, neglect, lack of resources, poor stability, and compromised perception of self-efficacy are just a few of the ways that hopelessness can manifest.

Adapting Frankl terms to this scenario, this is when one has an 'infected' will to meaning. As a pioneer of existential approaches to therapy, Frankl held that humans were happiest when they were able to find purpose and meaning in life. Using examples of inmates trapped in concentration camps, he often found that once people lost hope and found life to be meaningless, they quickly succumbed to the poor state of their health (illness, fatigue, starvation, etc.). This is a condition he called the existential vacuum; when an individual feels hopelessly trapped by emotional states like boredom, emptiness, loneliness, and life bears no meaning.

He warned that this was a strong predictor for suicidal behavior as well.

Frankl speaks to the power of hopelessness and its influence on life itself. A common currency used to trade in concentration camps was cigarettes. Frankl noted that prisoners received these as rewards for doing dangerous jobs and could trade them for privileges, such as:

> Soup... often a very real respite from starvation... When we saw a comrade smoking his own cigarettes, we knew he had given up faith in his strength to carry on, and, once lost, the will to live seldom returned.

This is one of several indicators of hopelessness that Frankl noticed during his years in those camps. Once the prisoner gave up the fight to survive, their will "seldom returned." But this haunting phrase mirrors the high consequence pain that millions of people all over the world experience every day within their fight through trauma, adversity, and mental illness. It also mirrors the journeys of the characters in *The Last of Us* universe.

On the other hand, those in concentration camps who found meaning in daily work, policing, caring for fellow inmates in the infirmary, or dreaming of what the future could bring, were more often those who survived. The word that Frankl consistently repeated in this book was *resilience*. When one is willing to be uncomfortable, has faith in intrapersonal resources, and is willing to do or experience something difficult with a sense of optimism, this indicates resilience.

In the inverse effect, an infected will to meaning can eat away at one's perceived purpose in life. This infection is bred at the intersection of intensive psycho-emotional distress, distorted implicit bias, mindlessness, impaired emotion regulation systems, weakened self-awareness, and cognitive distortions. It can manifest in a multitude of physiological, psychological, sociocultural, and spiritual forms. Posttraumatic stress disorder, depression, anxiety, substance abuse, eating disorders, process addictions, suicidality, cancer, and chronic illness are all instigated or exacerbated by existential suffering.

 CONCLUSION

Ultimately, the goal of this chapter was to provide an opportunity to reflect on *The Last of Us* through the lens resilience in the face of adversity. Whether from the perspective of main, side, or catalogued characters from *The Last of Us* collectibles (e.g. Ish in the abandoned tunnels with Henry and Sam), this universe is a profound example of how traumatic experiences can alter human reality and connection to the world around us. Trauma challenges one's core life assumptions which help to navigate daily living, but resilience enables one to overcome it.

Recognize that your external life (behaviors, habits, relationships, hobbies, etc.) mirror internal thoughts, emotions, and core beliefs. The quality of one's life is influenced directly by their will to meaning and what perceived purpose makes life matter. I encourage you to start a conversation around the neurological, physical, and psycho-emotional dynamics that impede or support your ability to thrive. Think about what you see in the world of these stories and about how they remind you of the ones in your heart, spirit, body, and mind. What about you is reflected in *The Last of Us* universe and what emotion does this leave within you? Does this universe speak to some of your core values? Which parts of these stories are you drawn to and why? What do these thoughts communicate about you overall?

Trauma truly can result in a shattering of one's worldview... In this outcome of a new worldview, there is no meaning, control, connection, safe place, or dependable individual. Owens & Parsons

Resilience is a trait directly connected to will to meaning. But ultimately, will to meaning defines one's willingness to live. The characters featured in *The Last of Us* are a beautiful representation of this concept, as they fight to survive in a world filled with death while constantly tapping into their inner well of resiliency to adapt along the way. Regardless of each character's choices and traits, they are a part of a larger conversation about how our internal world is expressed throughout our outer world, such as in our relationships, jobs, and choices we navigate. An infected will to meaning permeates into every fabric of life and wellness, leaving behind difficult feelings, such as sadness, anger, and fear. If left untreated, an infected will to meaning can chip away at hope while eliciting a fatal result, such as hopelessness — statistically identified by modern research as a significant indicator of addiction formation, mental illness onset, mental/physical decline, and suicide.

This is why examining interests in creative content— such as the international attraction to *The Last of Us* universe — can provide unique opportunities to better understand ourselves. Regardless of the way one chooses to engage with these stories, they offer a window to observe and evaluate thoughts, feelings, and actions in a more palatable way. Through the various retellings of these stories, one can assess values, morals, and deepest inner workings to better cultivate a life worth living. If people can better access their potential for resiliency, then they have a higher likelihood of overcoming adversity. These characters offer a window into a universe through which we can see our own. This allows one to feel seen and connected with the world while reminding that we are not alone —... and connection with others is the ultimate 'why.'

"...*Even the helpless victim of a hopeless situation, facing a fate he cannot change, may rise above himself, may grow beyond himself, and by so doing change himself. He may turn a personal tragedy into a triumph.*" (Frankl, 1992, p. 170)

About the Author

MELINDA KORTE (SHE/THEY) is a nationally Board-Certified Music Therapist and Licensed Professional Counselor in the state of Pennsylvania. She has 10 years of professional experience in healthcare and has worked across the United States with vastly diverse sociocultural and clinical demographics. Through her work as a clinical supervisor and Senior Allied Clinical Therapist for Penn Medicine's inpatient program (affiliated with the University of Pennsylvania), she specializes in recovery from Complex Post-Traumatic Stress Disorder as well as other severe forms of mental illness. Her professional passions lie in cultivating salutogenic, equitable, trauma-informed care systems which help people to find light in even their darkest moments and make changes that empower them to thrive.

References:

American Psychiatric Association (2022). *Diagnostic and Statistical Manual of Mental Disorders, Text Revision (DSM-5-TR)* (5th ed.). American Psychiatric Publishing, Inc..

Bean, A. M., Daniel, E. S., & Hays, S. A. (2020). Video Games: The New Mythology. In *Integrating geek culture into therapeutic practice: The clinician's guide to geek therapy* (pp. 25–38). essay, Leyline Publishing, Inc.

Corey, M. S., & Corey, G. (2020). *Becoming a Helper (8th ed.)*. Cengage Learning US. https://online.vitalsource.com/books/9780357427354

Frankl, V. (1992). *Man's search for meaning (4th Edition)*. Beacon Press.

Hume, M. (2023, January 15). *What to know about Cordyceps, the real fungus from the last of US - the ...* 'The Last of Us' zombie fungus is real, and it's found in health supplements. https://www.washingtonpost.com/video-games/2023/01/15/last-of-us-hbo-cordyceps/

Kottler, J. (2022). *On being a therapist.* Oxford University Press.

Lin, B. Q., & Li, S. P. (2011). Cordyceps as an Herbal Drug. In I. F. F. Benzie (Eds.) et. al., *Herbal Medicine: Biomolecular and Clinical Aspects.* (2nd ed.). CRC Press/Taylor & Francis.

Maté, G. (2018). *In the Realm of Hungry Ghosts: Close Encounters with Addiction.* https://www.amazon.com/Realm-Hungry-Ghosts-Encounters-Addiction/dp/155643880X

Miller, W. R., & Rollnick, S. (2013*). Motivational interviewing: Helping people change (3rd ed.).* Guilford Press.

Owens, E. & Parsons, R. (2018) *Crisis and Trauma Counseling*. Cognella, Inc.. https://online.vitalsource.com/books/818451A

Ruiz, D. M., Ruiz, D. J., & Mills, J. (2010). *The Fifth Agreement: A Practical Guide to Self-Mastery*. Amber-Allen Publishing.

Sue, D. W., Sue, D., Neville, H. A., & Smith, L. (2022). Counseling the Culturally Diverse (9th ed.). Wiley Professional Development (P&T). https://online.vitalsource.com/books/9781119861911

Tonkuş, B., Çalışkan, B., & Alagöz, E. (2022). The relationship between suicide and hopefulness of young adults age 18-30: A systematic review. *Journal of Psychiatric Nursing, 13*(3), 253–262. https://doi.org/10.14744/phd.2022.76993

Wintle P. (2023). Mutants and Zombies Everywhere! Or Villains, Violence, and Selfishness: Questions of Humanity in the Post-apocalyptic (Pandemic) Video Game. *Games and Culture*, 15554120231182802. https://doi.org/10.1177/15554120231182802

Yalom, I. (2009). *The Gift of Therapy*. HarperCollins.

Yalom, I. D. (2013). *Love's executioner: And other tales of psychotherapy*. Penguin.

SURVIVING THE ZOMBIE APOCALYPSE: EXAMINING WHAT *THE LAST OF US* TEACHES ABOUT STRUGGLE AND RISING ABOVE

KAT JAEGER AND TONY JAEGER

"Endure and Survive" —Savage Starlight

The worst of times bring out the worst in some people, and in others the very best. When everything looks bleak, whether on a personal level or a global scale, people do one thing extremely well: they survive. For millions of years, human beings have definitively accomplished this singular feat, and it is this fact that has instilled a bone-deep knowledge in every person on Earth that, no matter how dire the situation, there is *meaning* in survival. *The Last of Us* explores the theme of hope in a time of utter hopelessness.

When it was released in 2013, the thought of a pandemic ravaging the global population was a matter of fiction. Little did players know that the characters' resilience and the search for hope portrayed in *The Last of Us* would resonate so profoundly with the real-world challenges that would unfold in the years to come.

When the COVID-19 pandemic broke out in 2020 and the world shut down, many things played out eerily similarly to how it does in the game (though thankfully many much more of us survived COVID-19 than did the fungal pandemic in game). People began growing apart from one another — the rifts widening by social media, the endless political drama of the preceding years, and countless other factors that did little more than divide and frighten the masses. Then came the pandemic, and despite the fear and the hatred of the time, people came together in ways that were both uncharacteristic of the predominant culture and quintessentially *human*. Selfishness abounded in those years; people hoarded supplies and committed very real violence on one another to acquire those resources. Corporations gouged prices on essential goods, committing a more sinister kind of violence on the public. Hate groups sprouted up, spewing vitriol and worse. The, lockdowns happened, and many other people did something unexpected.

Communities of mothers came together and ensured that babies received formula, which had become impossible to reliably find. Citizens confined to their homes adjourned to their balconies nightly to come as close together as legally allowed, and sang songs together. Thousands of people built island resorts in the popular video game *Animal Crossing*, trading fruits and other goods, holding virtual gatherings and chatting, and even holding wedding celebrations all in a bright and cute world that provided the perfect escape — but that discussion is for a different book. In short, when the world was at its worst, the people maintained their hope.

It may be a gross understatement to say that the pandemic in *The Last of Us* was worse than the one we experienced with COVID-19, because the game's cordyceps outbreak left only a fraction of the world's population alive. In the game a player can travel in the continental United States for days without seeing evidence of another person's presence. We see the isolation and feeling of loss depicted in *The Last of Us* through the game's characters, who are forced to navigate a world in which death and danger lurk around every corner. Joel and Ellie's experiences with grief and loss reflect the experiences of many people who have lost loved ones. Joel's anger toward the world and those who caused the outbreak are mirrored in the frustration that many people feel towards the COVID-19 virus and its impact on their lives. Ellie's struggle to accept the reality of the world around her, and her attempts to bargain with fate, reflect the desperation and hopelessness that many people have felt during the pandemic.

It is not the gorgeous graphics of *The Last of Us*, nor the many Game of the Year awards it has received, that has made this game into the cultural phenomena that is has become. Ultimately the biggest draw of the game is the emotional resonance and impact of the story. It is the very real and raw exploration of grief and loss that, sadly, now everyone can personally relate to. It is the hope that people are kept safe and dear, reflected in Joel and Ellie's journey, that keeps gamers coming back.

 JOEL'S NARRATIVE JOURNEY THROUGH GRIEF AND LOSS

Joel is at the center of one of the most heart-wrenching prologues in any piece of media. During the first night of the violent outbreak of the pandemic, Joel's daughter dies in his arms — killed not by a zombie but by a normal, panicked human just trying to do his job. The audience does not see Joel process through the typical sequence of the stages of grief. Instead, the story leaves off while he is feeling the very first moment of denial as Sarah fades away, and picks up long after he had reached the acceptance stage. Joel survives. He copes with the rapidly changing world around him, doing his best to cope and function. When the story picks back up, Joel is a man that has only three things: his life, his meal vouchers, and his partner, Tess. He is the very incarnation of grim acceptance. The player does not directly see the resilience built through literal torture, or the years of work it took to become the man he is at the outset of his adventure — because the story of Joel's resilience is a bloody one.

Resilience science became a focal point for mental health researchers after World War II. People of all ages sought treatment for physical and mental trauma from a wide variety of causes, which led to enormous discoveries in the physiological and psychological mechanisms people use to deal with their stressors. According to scholar Romana Babić, resilience comes from simply continuing to function in unfavorable conditions and recovering from trauma despite one's unhappiness. Resilience is the result of combining risk factors and protective mechanisms to achieve positive growth. However, a person cannot become resilient without using their inborn ability to protect themselves from the stressors of the world. The ability to endure hardship is not given; it is earned the hard way. Only through exposure to potentially harmful circumstances can a person can cope with a situation and rise above struggle. The ability to develop resilience is hardwired into every person's DNA. This feature is part of what makes people such capable survivors.

Every single named character in *The Last of Us* is an example of where resilience can lead a person, for better and for worse. In the face of everything these characters go through, some become their best selves, bringing communities together for everyone's mutual benefit and survival, like Tommy and (at least at first) the Fireflies. Others, like David, lead groups with problematic motivations and actions. All the same, both Tommy and David survive the world around them and provide leadership to many in need, and save many more lives with their hopes for the future. In both cases, their methods are violent (even excessively so), but their willingness to face constant challenges inspires the people around them.

Over several decades, Tess forges relationships spanning geographically distant cities in a time when travel between them means almost certain death — and through those relationships is able to provide supplies to people in need. She sees the world fall apart, and responds by pulling together a community of people ready to work together despite potential danger. Joel sees the sun rise in the morning and faces every miserable day with the resolute belief that he will live to see it set. As he copes with the loss of his daughter and their future, Joel simply soldiers on with the unspoken hope of a brighter future. It is not until he meets Ellie that hope shows any indication of coming true.

DENIAL

At the outset of the main story of the game, Joel has seemingly processed through the stages of grief over Sarah's death. From the moment he meets Ellie, the player gets to experience Joel working through the stages firsthand as he copes with her presence in his life. These stages of grief were initially described by Elisabeth Kübler-Ross (1970) in her book *On Death and Dying*. The stages are denial, anger, bargaining, depression, and acceptance.

Denial is a defense mechanism used to distance oneself from a specific circumstance, where the individual simply cannot believe the event has occurred. Like a warm blanket protects a person from the harsh cold, denial insulates a person's psyche. In times of great stress, the part of the brain that processes the world around us shuts down due to the shock of the event. We see this phenomenon following traumatic events such as car crashes, diagnoses of terminal disease, and many other life-shattering events. Denial presents differently for each individual, but in every case the person is unable to reach understanding of the event is out of reach. They feel as though the trauma cannot possibly be happening to them.

The prologue of *The Last of Us* ends with Joel holding his daughter, in the throes of denial, — begging, pleading with Sarah not to go. Tommy understands what is happening, though he is clearly shaken by the truth of the situation, and does everything he could to help his brother through the moment. Joel, however, can only see the extent of Sarah's wound, but cannot access the rational part of his brain that probably recognizes just how severe it is. In the moment, Joel's survival mechanisms kick in t to numb the agony of the situation as the camera fades to black.

ANGER

Once the reality of the situation sets in, a person commonly feels anger or resentment, and not only toward the person lost or the traumatic situation itself. Trauma can change the trajectory of a person's entire life, and it makes sense that person will grieve over the loss of the future they had envisioned. The bitterness of the loss can spiral out of control. Anger leads to hate, and hate leads to suffering.

In life and in *The Last of Us,* we are reminded that life is not fair. At no point is this clearer than in the face of traumatic events or loss, which are also the worst times for this understanding to crystallize. However, mental health practitioners encourage sufferers to be *present* in their anger and feel it fully. Following the unreality of denial, anger grounds a person as it brings the reality of the situation into full focus. The situation *is* unfair, and it is also necessary to understand and feel those feelings to cope and heal.

It is easy for a person to dwell in anger for an extended period of time. The player is only given an incomplete, secondhand account of Joel's process of going through the other stages of grief, and it is arguably a good thing that the player does not accompany him on that bloody journey. The world becomes a place where Joel can put his pain and anger to good use, and therefore deprives him of the opportunity to process his grief in a healthy way.

BARGAINING

Anger puts the traumatic event into harsh perspective, but it still can also function as a kind of denial. According to resilience science, human beings are hard-wired to survive our stressors, to become hardened to them. As a species, we are rebels. Some of the greatest works in human history have come from defiance in the face of incredible odds. A person's likely reaction to being told something is impossible is to raise their chin and say, "Watch me." Anger and denial feel in the parts of ourselves where we are still primal beings — but we are also creatures of reason and logic, and cannot hide from the truth forever. Eventually a person must confront the truth, and with that confrontation comes desperation; an attempt to tempt fate or a higher power into a bargain to bring back what once was theirs yours.

From the moment of Joel and Ellie's first meeting, Joel is visibly agitated and often angry about the predicament he finds himself in. A reportedly simple escort mission tears open decades-old wounds, leading him to several desperate attempts to avoid the job regardless the payment he would receive. Every friendly face Joel meets throughout the game is someone he tries to convince to take Ellie the rest of the way to the Fireflies. He tries to strike every bargain he can to avoid taking responsibility for Ellie's continued safety, because the pain of having to face the grief she awakens in him is too much to bear. Joel holds onto denial, which allows him to believe he might be able to avoid doing the job. The truth comes for him as it comes for everyone who grieves.

 DEPRESSION

Depression sets in as the full weight of the burden of loss comes into focus. The defense mechanisms meant to shelter us from the worst of the pain melt away in the face of the simple truth of the situation, and the time comes to *feel* the natural feelings that come with loss. Echoes of the past dance around inside the mind, and Earth's gravity doubles to drag us down, and colors fade into a joyless void. Depression is the opposite of the manic energy of the anger and bargaining stages of grief; it leaves a person exhausted and hopeless.

One of the coping mechanisms that Joel develops is an avoidant attachment to people to keep his emotions safe in a time when such feelings were considered secondary to survival. While working through the depression stage, it is easy to detach from the world, and from previous attachments to people or activities or hobbies. While processing his grief over losing Sarah, Joel removes himself entirely from almost everyone. While he keeps most people emotionally at arm's length, that is twice as true for Ellie, who reminds him of his daughter. At every stage of the early game, Joel is emotionally distant and he often directs annoyance at her even when he is clearly amused, just to drive home the point that he wants to keep her at an emotional distance, and she should not get attached.

The depression stage can lead a person to self-destructive behaviors. They question where the value is in continuing to live when the world seems to bring more pain day after day. In Tommy's mountain village, when Joel finally convinces Tommy to take Ellie on and he seemed free to rid himself of his burden, his mood continues to darken. Joel fears he will lose Ellie during their journey together, and in his attempt to protect himself from more hurt he ends up causing himself that very pain.

 ACCEPTANCE

Every dark tunnel has a light at the very end, and the only way a person can discover it is to pass through the tunnel. In the pitch blackness of depression, it can be deceptively easy to believe that nothing can assuage the pain. The most empathetic, gifted, certified therapist or grief counselor can only provide skills or tools to help a person cope with the depression, but it is up to the person grieving to feel and process their emotions.

In time, depression, anger, and denial fade away and make room for stability. Attempts to bargain with fate become hollower as the new reality sets in. The realization that things will never return to the way they were is not a good thing, but it is this realization that allows the person to move forward.

Someone can experience the most crushing loss and *still* move forward. Nothing can take away the pain, but all things fade away in time, including the suffering caused by trauma and loss. In every chapter of *The Last of Us*, Joel shows his longing for his lost daughter h decades after her death, and he grows through his struggles and builds a relationship with Ellie that nourishes him emotionally. His grief becomes tolerable through the rare moments of vulnerability and connection and genuine warmth shared between them. The acceptance stage is not freedom from the pain of loss, it is merely the emotional fulfillment of what a person needs to move forward from it.

Leading up to the final scene of the game, and as he had done in the years following Sarah's death, Joel faces his trauma, shoulders his pain, and accepts the mantle of responsibility for Ellie's safety. The culmination of his years of violence, trauma, and loss came down to the hope that Ellie and the Firefly scientists can fix the broken world — and, Joel hopes, himself. A switch is flipped and acceptance sets in to allow a measure of peace.

 ELLIE'S RESILIENCE

Ellie's resilience is not merely a response to the loss she has experienced in her life. It comes from genuine awe of the world before her birth, and hope for what she believes it will be again. While Joel's hope sprouts from the disbelief that he will live to see a better world, by the time the player meets Ellie, her own hope has bloomed in the very real possibility that she will be part of restoring the world to its former glory.

No stranger to grief, Ellie lost both of her parents and best friend, among many others. Throughout the game she rails against the simple, often grim, truth of her life to that point — that everybody goes away eventually. The audience watches Ellie move through the stages of grief time and again throughout the game. Because she was raised in a turbulent environment, her ability to navigate grief seems almost natural. This ease does not lessen the pain she feels or the depth of her sorrow, but grief does not what define her. The harsh reality of her world forced her to persevere through loss from the earliest of age. Joel's character arc is defined by his own loss years before Ellie's birth. Ellie, by contrast, is characterized by her hope and grit in the face of mortal danger every day.

 ENDURE AND SURVIVE

Ellie clings to the little things that keep her day worth living, focusing more on those glimmers of hope rather than her triggers. Without the little boosts of joy from her joke book or the rare opportunity to dig into a new *Savage Starlight* comic, it is possible that Ellie might not have muster the strength to persevere. The phrase "endure and survive" is littered throughout the game, underlining Ellie's story arc. A person navigating the Kübler-Ross stages of grief is in the process of developing resilience, forming the neural pathways that help a person to navigate loss in the future. Without going through the steps in one form or another, developing that grit is difficult, if not outright impossible. But Ellie's story is not about suffering or loss. Hers is a story of what comes after the processing of grief, and the maintenance of hope.

Despite unfathomable trauma throughout her formative years, Ellie can rise above the pain and unfairness of the world she lives in, and does her best to maintain a positive attitude. Every day is filled with struggle and exhaustion, but she approaches her difficulties head on, steadfast in her belief that she will be instrumental in saving the world. The key is that the belief that she would save the world gives her *purpose*, a reason to keep putting one foot in front of the other.

Napoleon Bonaparte once quipped that a person would do anything for a scrap of colored ribbon; meaning that if you give a person a purpose, something meaningful to dedicate their life to, they will rise above all other challenges in the pursuit of that mission. Starting a few days before she met Joel, Ellie's very real purpose in her life is to find the Fireflies and in so doing, save the world. With that goal on the horizon, how could any challenge be too great to overcome?

As summarized by researcher Margarida Pocinho, pursuing a goal can help drive positive outcomes in overcoming difficulties. Setting one's sights on a higher meaning or purpose — while simultaneously facing difficulties — can reduce stress levels and improve overall physical and psychological well-being. Every step forward Ellie takes is one she faces, not with grim determination like Joel, but with hope. The knowledge that her struggles will all be worthwhile make every struggle and brush with death more manageable. This knowledge also helps her adapt to and move forward from every challenge, instead of being beaten down by her trauma. Ellie needed to grow up strong, and develop grit from a very young age, but it is her sense of purpose that keeps her head held high.

A person's purpose does not have to be as grand as Ellie's; very few people are called to save the world, but everyone benefits from keeping a goal or task on the horizon to focus on when times get tough. The specific goal matters less than its ability to motivate. People improve themselves through effort, and as each person achieves personal growth, the difficulties in the world around them become easier to manage. I

ENDURE AND SURVIVE AND ... THRIVE

Despite the constant danger in her life, especially after leaving her home in the Quarantine Zone, Ellie's journey is filled with discovery. Every turn in the cross-country road she takes holds danger, but she just cannot help but be enthralled by the world around her. On their journey to find the Fireflies, Ellie is fascinated by the majestic remnants of a lost world she will never know. Ellie and Joel navigate felled skyscraper office buildings, discover shabby homes in sewers, and explore abandoned university campuses, and though these locales were familiar and often mundane to Joel, Ellie never fails to see the beauty behind the danger. Every new building has places to explore, trinkets to figure out, and relics to discover. In her eyes, Joel is every bit as much a relic of that world as her *Savage Starlight* comics, and she takes every opportunity to learn as much as she can from Joel. Her curiosity drives her, and gives her resilience against the horror witnesses throughout the game.

The Last of Us games are good at many things, chief among them is bringing tears to the eyes of the player. In the beginning of the game, it breaks the player's heart. At the end of the game, it makes hearts sing. One scene captures this perfectly. Toward the end of the game, Ellie's wonder is rewarded with a truly memorable moment when she gets to meet a herd of giraffes. Released from the city zoo when humans could no longer care for them, the giraffes not only survived the apocalypse, but thrive within it — and in that moment serve as a symbol of her own survival. The scene is breathtaking, watching tenderness blossom in Ellie, like a flower growing through concrete, as she interacts with the giraffe. She was raised in the hardest world imaginable, had to become brave and unspeakably tough, yet she remains open to trust and vulnerability when the giraffe gives her the same. For many, tenderness and vulnerability are kept behind walls built of pain and trauma, but expressing and feeling these things — as Ellie models for us — can be tremendously useful to the healing process.

 CONCLUSION

Not everybody has to save the world, or even to protect the one who would but everyone does have the tools to face their struggles as if they did. No matter the struggle you are facing, you have the strength and willpower to face it down and overcome it. It is baked into your DNA. Hope is your birthright and it is everyone's job to cultivate it, even in the face of a literal zombie apocalypse. It is the willingness to face fears head on that makes a person grow stronger. Remember that resilience is an adaptation that is brought on by stress. There are many sources of resilience shown in *The Last of Us*, and powerful examples of the human ability to overcome the unimaginable. The more, and more diverse, stressors you face, the more tools and ammunition you develop to handle them. You wrap up your wounds a little bit faster each time, and you learn how to move just a little bit better through your environment. Becoming more powerful is a gradual process. Every story has an end, and everyone has the tools to work toward The Good Ending.

About the Authors

KAT JAEGER (SHE/HER), Licensed Clinical Mental Health Counselor, is the co-founder of a forthcoming therapy practice dedicated to providing innovative mental health services. Specializing in working with children, teenagers, and young adults, Kat focuses on ADHD and anxiety, offering compassionate support and guidance to her clients. Beyond her clinical work, Kat is a passionate advocate for neurodivergent affirming care and promoting awareness of the mental health benefits of video games and therapeutic animals. As the owner of Happy Pixels, Kat works to help therapists use video games in therapy and consult as a mental health consultant on video games. With the upcoming launch of her practice, Kat will further her mission by incorporating geek/video game therapy and therapeutic animals into her practice. Through her dedication and innovative approach, Kat seeks to create a more inclusive and understanding environment for mental health. Outside of work, Kat enjoys spending time with her therapy dog, playing video games, and Saturday adventures in the community with her spouse.

Author of Fowl Play and Chef, **TONY JAEGER**'S dark satirical stories do their best to help the reader look at the world differently than before. Tony lives in Utah with his wife and a menagerie of furry animals. He is an avid video game and Magic: the Gathering player, and absolutely loves cheese.

References

Babić, R., Rastovic, P., Babić, M., Ćurlin, M., & Šimić, J. (2020). *Resilience in health and illness - psychiatria danubina*. Psychiatria Danubina. https://www.psychiatria-danubina.com/UserDocsImages/pdf/dnb_vol32_noSuppl%202/dnb_vol32_noSuppl%202_226.pdf

Kübler-Ross, E. (1970). On death and dying. Collier Books/Macmillan Publishing Co.

Pocinho M, Garcês S, Popa D. Editorial: Positive Psychology in Everyday Life. Front Psychol. 2022 Jun 1;13:913569. doi: 10.3389/fpsyg.2022.913569. PMID: 35719469; PMCID: PMC9199901.

READY TO JOURNEY INTO THE

Checkpoints & Autosaves
By the time you reach the last page, you will have a guide to finding common ground with your child that will help you as a parent foster a better relationship, and maybe a new favorite hobby.

Final Fantasy
The Psychology of Final Fantasy guides gamers on a real-world quest of self-discovery so that they can surpass their own limit break.

Dungeons & Dragons
The Psychology of Dungeons & Dragons, is relevant to players, game masters, and even game designers. It applies decades of established and cutting-edge research to help readers understand how playing the game drives behaviors, shapes play, impacts relationships, and changes players once they put away the dice.

Bluey
Through expert commentary, character studies, and thematic explorations, "The Psychology of Bluey" reveals how the show's nuanced portrayal of everyday life can teach us about patience, understanding, and the joy found in life's simplest moments.

My Hero Academia
The Psychology of My Hero Academia" offers a distinctive and contemplative exploration, catering to devoted fans of the series and those intrigued by the psychological impact of storytelling.

Geek Therapy Card Deck
The Geek Therapy Card Deck helps people find balance, reduce stress, bring awareness into their lives, and be mindful in the moment allowing them to manage distress, regulate their emotions and understand life relationships using Geek Cultural Artifacts and insights found within.

GEEK PSYCHOLOGY SERIES?

Meme Life
This book seeks to explain how memes influence societies and cultures.

Pokémon
The Psychology of Pokémon guides gamers on a real-world quest of self-discovery to unravel the mysteries of the Pokémon series.

Elden Ring
Few games have loomed as large in popular video game culture in recent years as Elden Ring, a devastatingly difficult sword-and-sorcery RPG that became a bestseller when it launched on PC, PlayStation, and Xbox consoles back in February 2022.

Gamers Journey
In video games, we are asked to travel through breathtaking virtual creations, all the while collecting a limitless experience which we are fortunate enough to see, hear, and move through as we feel the unleashed joy of our play. This book will bring you through that journey yourself.

The Witcher
Uncover the secrets behind the complex motivations and behaviors of Geralt of Rivia, Yennefer of Vengerberg, and other iconic characters in this captivating exploration of the acclaimed fantasy series.

The Last of Us
In "The Psychology of The Last of Us," delve deep into the hauntingly profound narrative and characters of the groundbreaking video game that captured the hearts and minds of players worldwide.

Visit our website for the full collection of Geek Psychology Series: **shop.geektherapeutics.com**